John P Breckenridt

XHY$7 50

THE THIRD FORCE

FRANK G. GOBLE

THE
THIRD
FORCE

*The Psychology of
Abraham Maslow*

Foreword by Abraham Maslow

GROSSMAN PUBLISHERS

New York, 1970

Additional acknowledgments for the use of copyrighted material will be found on pp. 193–195, which are hereby made part of this copyright page. The author wishes to express his gratitude to all publishers and authors for their cooperation in giving him permission to quote from copyrighted material. Any errors or omissions that may have inadvertently occurred will be corrected in any subsequent printings upon notification to the author.

Second Printing

Published by Grossman Publishers, Inc.
125A East 19th Street, New York, N. Y. 10003
Published simultaneously in Canada by
Fitzhenry and Whiteside, Ltd.
Manufactured in the United States.
Library of Congress Catalogue Card Number: 71–114940.

To my wife, Margaret

Foreword

I am very happy that Mr. Goble has done so well what I have often wanted to do but couldn't. He has brought together into a systematized and simplified organization what is, after all, an unstructured sprawl of writing, far too much to expect any but professional students to read. This kind of abstracting, condensing, and simplifying so that the essential structure shows through clearly is an uncommon talent. Mr. Goble has it, and I do not.

I am, of course, very gratified that he found my writings to be worthy of this effort. I am also pleased that through this book I shall be able to speak to an audience larger and more inclusive than the psychologists to whom I have usually addressed myself.

I want to stress that any one of a dozen theorists would have been quite as useful as a representative of Third Force Psychology. This is precisely one important aspect of this new World-View—that it is a Zeitgeist, a spirit of the age, a change of basic thinking along the total front of man's endeavors, a potential change in every social institution, in every one of the "fields" of intellectual endeavor, and in every one of the professions. Therefore, as a movement it has no single leader, no one great name by which to characterize it. Most revolutions in World-View have been char-terized by the name of a single person; for example: the Freudians, the Darwinians, the Newtonians, the Marxians, the Copernicans, the Einsteinians, etc.

In contrast, the Third Force (or Humanistic Psychology), which is developing a new image of man, is the work of *many* men. Not only this, but it is also paralleled by independent advances and discoveries in other fields as well. Thus, there is rapidly developing a new image of society and of all its institutions. So, also, is there a new philosophy of science, of education, of religion, of psychotherapy, of politics, of economics, etc., etc., etc. Taken together these developments can be called single aspects of a comprehensive philosophy of *everything*.

So far the word "Humanistic" is being used most widely as a label for this all-embracing synthesis and for all its separable aspects. I don't know whether this name will stick or not. It's now being strained by its own inner dynamics, which are already generating a psychology and philoso-phy of the person-transcending (transpersonal) and of the humanness-transcending (transhuman). These newer developments come from *within* Humanistic Psychology, generated inexorably out of its own theoretical and empirical necessities. I am tempted to call it a pregnancy within a pregnancy because this Humanistic Psychology is itself not yet fully born as a science, let alone matured.

Clearly the next step for this psychology and philosophy is research, research, research—not only in the laboratory but, more importantly, in the field, in society, in factories, homes, hospitals, communities, even nations. I should say that I include under the rubric of research the type of life "experiments" and field "experiments" that Mr. Goble has sampled in the second part of his book—and which he knows much more of than I do. One can learn from these attempts to apply a not-yet-verified theory, watching it carefully to see how well it works or doesn't work.

Abraham H. Maslow

Contents

Preface

This book will present a condensation of the ideas of Dr. Abraham Maslow, one of our nation's most distinguished psychologists. Garnered from his five books, over one hundred reports, essays, magazine articles, and speeches, the book will present Dr. Maslow's ideas in language understandable to the layman. Students and busy professionals will find it a valuable starting point for a more detailed study of the original documents. It is a book for everyone who is interested in human beings and their behavior.

Former professor of psychology at Brandeis University, and former president of the American Psychological Association, Dr. Maslow is presently Resident Fellow at the Laughlin Foundation in Menlo Park, California.*

He has developed a new, comprehensive theory of human motivation which touches on every aspect of human behavior. It is a theory which challenges some of the basic premises that have dominated American behavior theory for at least the last four or five decades. Called "Third

* Abraham Maslow died suddenly of a heart attack on June 8, 1970, shortly after he prepared the Foreword for this book.

Force Psychology"—a name Dr. Maslow coined to distinguish his work and that of others from the two other major theories of human behavior (Freudianism and Behaviorism), the new theory is centered on man himself—his needs, his goals, his achievements, his success.

When plans for this book were first announced and we requested help in identifying applications of Third Force in action, we were deluged with material from Dr. Maslow's friends and supporters from all over the world. Most of the material was excellent and pertinent, but the demands of space were such that we could not use all of it. We want to thank those friends and colleagues of Dr. Maslow who contributed information and suggestions, and all those whose work is described in the second part of this book. We owe special thanks to the friends and staff of the Thomas Jefferson Research Center who contributed so much time and effort to this book—particularly Ordway Tead, Henry Geiger, and James Yates, for their help in reading the manuscript and offering suggestions; Peggy Granger, for her faithful editorial assistance; Mary Smulo, Amelia Manning and AlVerna Taylor, for their secretarial and typing help; and Daphne Alley, for her valuable assistance in accumulating research data. We wish to express appreciation to the publishers of Dr. Maslow's previous books and articles who have given their permission for frequent quotations.

Most particularly, of course, we wish to thank Dr. Maslow himself, without whose help and encouragement the book would not have been possible. He furnished constant supervision and suggestions for the manuscript in progress and read and corrected the final draft.

At this time of world turmoil and apparently insoluble social problems, readers will find Dr. Maslow's ideas stimulating, encouraging, and hopeful. It is my personal conviction, and it is one shared by many others, that the Third Force theory of psychology represents a major breakthrough that is capable of changing the course of world history.

Frank Goble

THE THIRD FORCE

PART ONE

PART ONE

CHAPTER I

Historical Perspective

Prior to the 19th Century the study of human behavior was almost exclusively the province of theologians and philosophers. Sparked by the discoveries of Galileo, Isaac Newton, and the scientists who followed them, concern about man and his behavior began gradually to shift from the theologian to the scientist. Wilhelm Wundt (1832–1920) has generally been credited with founding scientific psychology. He published a general handbook of the new science and founded the first formal laboratory of psychology at Leipzig, Germany in 1879. He started the first journal devoted to experimental psychology in 1881.

Other schools of psychological thought were soon introduced—William James developed Functionalism in America, Gestalt Psychology was founded in Germany, Freud's Psychoanalysis began in Vienna, and John B. Watson started Behaviorism in America.

By 1954 when Maslow published his book, *Motivation and Personality*, there were two major theories dominant in American universities. While there were numerous splinter theories, the majority of psychiatrists, psychologists, and behavioral scientists could trace their thinking to either Sigmund Freud or John B. Watson.

Freudianism

Sigmund Freud (1856–1939) advanced one of recent history's most comprehensive and influential theories of human behavior. "Anyone who reached adulthood prior to 1950," says Hobart Mowrer, former president of the American Psychological Association, "knows how pervasively Freudian theory and practice dominated not only the specific field of psychotherapy, but also education, jurisprudence, religion, child rearing, and art, literature, and social philosophy." [1]

Richard La Piere, Stanford sociologist, wrote in 1959, "It (the Freudian ethic) has become the ethic that is most commonly advocated by the intellectual leaders of the United States." [2]

The subject of controversy from the publication in 1900 of his first major work, *The Interpretation of Dreams*, Freud was a pioneer, dedicating himself to solving the problems of the mentally ill. His work, to some extent, was a reaction to the overemphasis on will power and rational man. A prolific writer, he altered his theories as he gained new data, but certain central ideas have remained relatively unchanged. He rejected not only the methods of theology, but the conclusions as well. To Freud the so-called religious experience was a childish delusion.

Greatly influenced by the work of Darwin, his starting premise was that man was the product of accidental evolution. Living matter resulted from and evolved through the action of cosmic forces upon inorganic matter. Man was an animal and only an animal. In his words, "In the course of his development toward culture, man acquired a dominating position over his fellow creatures in the animal kingdom. Not content with this supremacy, however, he began to place a gulf between his nature and theirs. He denied the possession of reason to them, and to himself he attributed an immortal soul, and made claims to a divine descent which permitted him to annihilate the bond of community between him and the animal kingdom. . . . We all know that, little more than half a century ago, the researches of Charles Darwin, his collaborators, and predecessors put an end to this presumption on the part of man. Man is not a being different from animals or superior to them; he himself originates in the animal race and is related more closely to some of its members and more distantly to others." [3]

Throughout his career Freud hoped to reduce human behavior to chemical and physical dimensions. His interest was the mentally disturbed and his laboratory, his mental patients. Freud had little interest in the social implications of his theories, although there were many. He called attention to the unconscious mind and its influence on human behavior, comparing the mind to an iceberg with the tip, or conscious portion, a tiny fraction as compared with the submerged, or unconscious part.

Acquired from his animal origin were man's basic, genetic, instinctual drives. These could be divided into two major categories: the life instinct for survival and propagation, of which the sex drive was the most important. Freud's dictum was "the goal of all life is death." [4] These unconscious animal instincts which he called the "id," were powerful, anti-social, and irrational. "These instincts fill it (the id) with energy, but it has no organization and no unified will, only an impulsion to obtain satisfaction for the instinctual needs, in accordance with the pleasure principle. The laws of logic—above all, the laws of contradiction—do not hold for processes in the id. Contradictory impulses exist side by side. . . . Naturally, the id knows no values, no good and evil, no morality." [5]

Freud believed that man was in constant conflict with himself and society. The virtuous person was one who repressed his impulses, while a sinful person enjoyed them. He described psychoanalysis as a "dynamic conception which reduces mental life to the interplay of reciprocally urging and checking forces." [4] Man's raw instincts were repressed by the artificially-imposed customs and morals of his society. This acquired veneer of responsibility, which Freud called super-ego, was interpreted and imposed on the child by his parents. The id and the super-ego were constantly at war with one another, and the resulting behavior came from man's ego, that part of his mind which combined the forces of the id and super-ego to determine action.

In *New Introductory Lectures on Psychoanalysis*, Freud spoke of the basic hostility of men toward one another. "Culture has to call up every possible reinforcement to erect barriers against the aggressive instincts of men . . . hence, too, its ideal command to love one's neighbor as oneself, which is really justified by the fact that nothing is so completely at variance with human nature as this." [6]

Or, there is his statement, "Hatred is at the bottom of all the relations of affection and love between human beings; hatred in relation to objects is older than love." [7]

Freud held that the basic direction of man's life was generally determined at an early age (about five years), although it did occasionally change and could be altered by psychoanalysis, the Freudian method of therapy. Moral behavior, good behavior, unselfish behavior was unnatural, but could occur when the individual learned to repress or redirect his id. Freud called this "sublimation." Mental illness was the result of a super ego or a moral code that was too unrealistic and the patient's inability to cope with the resulting conflict.

The orthodox procedure in psychoanalysis is free association and dream analysis. The patient relaxes on a couch and is encouraged to talk about whatever enters his mind, and, also, to talk about his dreams.

Freud found that, given the right conditions, the patient soon began to talk about memories of early childhood experiences and these, together with dream interpretations, provided the therapist with insight into the patient's personality and how it developed. Through reduction of guilt and by developing an ability to redirect or sublimate his repressed desire, the patient was to conquer his mental disturbance.

Today, although there is no widely accepted alternate theory used by psychiatrists, few adhere strictly to Freudian doctrine.

Behaviorism

What might be called the "second" force in behavioral science is the work of those relating most closely to the theory of Behaviorism. This general theory was formulated by John B. Watson (1878-1958) just after the turn of the century. Watson was a professor of psychology at Johns Hopkins University. He sought to make the study of man as objective and scientific as possible—like Freud, he sought to reduce man's behavior to chemical and physical terms.

The term "Behaviorism" is now used generally to describe the work of a number of related theories of psychology, sociology, and behavioral sciences covering the work of, not only John Watson, but also Edward Thorndike, Clark Hull, John Dollard, Neal Miller, B.F. Skinner, and many others. Predecessors of this line of reasoning were Isaac Newton, who developed the scientific method in the physical sciences, and Charles Darwin, who proposed that man was the result of a process of accidental evolution from lower animals.

Freud's theory was developed primarily from listening to his patients and from his subjective interpretation of their neuroses. The Behaviorists concentrated on the strictly objective "scientific" approach. Also, Freud placed the major motivational emphasis on deep inner drives and urges; the Behaviorists placed the emphasis on external, environmental influences. Nothing of the subjective was included in their theorizing. Said Watson, "The Behaviorist dropped from his scientific vocabulary all subjective terms such as sensation, perception, image, desire, purpose, and even thinking and emotion as they were subjectively defined." [8]

John Watson was particularly influenced by the work of the Russian psychologist, Ivan Pavlov, who demonstrated that dogs would salivate whenever they heard a tuning fork, even though they received no meat. This was called "conditioned reflex."

Behaviorists put great stress on this associative or stimulus-response learning as the major explanation for human behavior. The difference between Freud's theory, emphasizing inner drives of man, and the Behaviorists' reliance on "outer" or environmental influences on man can be clearly seen.

"Personality is the sum of activities that can be discovered by actual observation of behavior over a long enough time to give reliable information," Watson said. "In other words, personality is but the end product of our habit systems." [8]

A basic assumption is that there is no scientific basis for morality. Thus, the position is one of moral and cultural relativism. "The Behaviorist is not interested in his (man's) morals, except as a scientist; in fact, he doesn't care what kind of a man he is." [8] Man is flexible, malleable, and a passive victim of his environment, which determines his behavior.

The early years are the important ones—on this point, virtually all schools of psychology agree. From this came the recommendation that parents should maintain a permissive, gratifying, undemanding attitude toward children in the early years; particularly in regard to feeding, toilet-training, early sex training, and attempts to control anger and aggression. Any frustration at this time was believed to produce a tendency toward adult neurosis.

This point of view is summarized by two current co-authors, Gardner Lindzey and Calvin Hall, who have analyzed and compared the various theories of personality. They describe the work of two contemporary Behaviorists: "Dollard and Miller assume that unconscious conflict, learned for the most part during infancy and childhood, serves as the basis for most severe emotional problems in later life. They agree with psychoanalytic theorists in considering experiences of the first half dozen years of life crucial determinants of adult behavior. It is important to realize that neurotic conflict is not only learned by the child but it is learned primarily as the result of conditions created by the parent." [4]

In the early 1930s the Institute of Human Relations at Yale University sought to coordinate the disciplines of psychology, psychiatry, sociology, and anthropology. Under the leadership of Clark L. Hull, an enthusiastic proponent of Behaviorism, this was the center for a distinguished group of behavioral scientists. Under Hull's influence the Institute exerted a powerful and enduring influence on a generation of young social scientists.

In his interesting book on the history of ideas, *The Broken Image*, Floyd W. Matson quotes Watson by saying, "In short, the cry of the Behaviorist is, 'Give me the baby and my world to bring it up in and I'll make it crawl and walk: I'll make it climb and use its hands in constructing buildings of stone or wood; I'll make it a thief, a gunman, or a dope fiend. The possibility of shaping in any direction is almost endless.'" [9]

Like Freud and like Darwin before him, the Behaviorists saw man as merely another type of animal, with no essential differences from animals and with the same destructive, anti-social tendencies. In his book, *Behaviorism*, Watson stated, "We believed then (1912) as we do now, that man is an animal, different from other animals only in the types of behavior he displays." [8] And, "the extent to which most of us are shot through with a savage background is almost unbelievable." [8]

B. F. Skinner, Harvard psychologist and present day advocate and leader in the Behaviorist tradition, says "The only differences I expect to see revealed between the behavior of rats and man (aside from enormous differences in complexity) lie in the field of verbal behavior." [9] Because of the belief in the essential similarity of man and animals, because of convenience, and for reasons of objectivity, Behaviorist psychologists have based much of their work on animal experimentation.

Ethics, morals, and values are only the result of associative learning.

The only true measure of right and wrong is the survival of the culture. "A scientific analysis may lead us to resist the more immediate blandishments [sic] of freedom, justice, knowledge, or happiness in considering the long-run consequences of survival," says Skinner. ". . . The hypothesis that man is not free is essential to the application of scientific method to the study of human behavior." [9]

While the work of Sigmund Freud and many other psychiatrists and psychologists concerned with mental health rested primarily upon clinical observation, the Behaviorist emphasized carefully controlled laboratory experiments. From early in this century until the present time, the bulk of experimental work in the United States by psychologists, social scientists, and others has concentrated on developing scientific evidence. Professors Calvin Hall and Gardner Lindzey stated in 1957, "The application of stimulus response concepts to behavioral events outside the laboratory has taken place, for the most part, during the past 25 or 30 years. *In this interval* a very large amount of relevant empirical research has accumulated. Furthermore, a number of able young psychologists have been trained during recent years, particularly at Yale and the University of Iowa, who possess the technical skill and theoretical conviction necessary to increase enormously the existing stock of such empirical evidence. The recent past has witnessed not only an empirical boom in this area but also the appearance of a large number of individuals actively concerned with extending and modifying the concepts we have discussed." [4]

The continued major influence of this general point of view is documented in a more recent statement by Floyd W. Matson, 1966. "The demonstrable truth is, . . . that the basic tenets of Behaviorism have not only been kept alive in the laboratories of experimentalists but hold as secure and prominent a position as ever in their conceptual schemes. Moreover, it is hardly too much to say that the most militant leadership of a general movement of Behavioral science has been furnished by the advocates of its thriving namesake in psychology." [9] Still more recently (1968), a distinguished panel of scholars, representing a first-hand knowledge of behavioral-science trends in England, Europe, India, Africa, and Australia, concluded that the trend in these countries was away from Freudianism towards Behaviorism. (Sixth annual meeting of American Associates of Humanistic Psychology, August 27-29, 1968, San Francisco, California.)

CHAPTER 2

The Third Force

Who Was Abraham Maslow?

As a boy Abraham Maslow was the only Jewish boy in a non-Jewish
Brooklyn suburb. He has said that it was a little like being the first Negro
in an all-white school. Considering that Maslow today is one of the most
popular men in his field—seldom the target of the slings and arrows
hurled by other disagreeing psychologists—it is hard to believe him when
he says, "I was isolated and unhappy. I grew up in libraries and among
books, almost without friends." [1]

As the young Maslow matured he began to appreciate the works of such
philosophers as Alfred North Whitehead, Henri Bergson, Thomas Jefferson, Abraham Lincoln, Plato, and Spinoza. He described the discovery of
William Graham Sumner's *Folkways* as a "Mount Everest in my life." [1]

Far from having spent all his early years in cloistered study, however,
Maslow had experience in the practical world as well. (This is, doubtless,
part of the reason for the mature Maslow's practical recommendations.)
He started working very early—first delivering newspapers. He spent

many summers working for the family company which, incidentally his
brothers still run. It is today a large and successful barrel-manufacturing
corporation; Universal Containers, Inc.

He married early—when he was twenty and his wife nineteen. "Life
didn't really start for me until I got married and went to Wisconsin," he
says. "I had discovered J. B. Watson, and I was sold on Behaviorism. It
was an explosion of excitement for me." [1] He studied monkeys there under
the guidance of Professor Harry Harlow, and wrote his doctorate on the
sexual and dominance characteristics of monkeys.

However, as his reading of Gestalt and Freudian psychology grew, so
his enthusiasm for Behaviorism began to wane. And when the young Maslows began their family, Abraham Maslow made an important discovery.
"Our first baby changed me as a psychologist," he writes, "It made the
behaviorism I had been so enthusiastic about look so foolish I could not
stomach it anymore. It was impossible." [2] "I looked at this tiny, mysterious
thing," he told Mary Harrington Hall in an interview for the journal *Psychology Today*, "and felt so stupid. I was stunned by the mystery and by
the sense of not really being in control . . . I'd say that anyone who had a
baby couldn't be a Behaviorist." [1]

The thirties found the Maslows back in New York, where he was a
professor of psychology at Brooklyn College.

New York City at that time was a very special place—Maslow has called
it the center of the psychological universe. It was here that he received the
most profound learning experience of his life. "I never met Freud or
Jung," he writes, "but I did meet with Adler in his home, where he used to
run Friday night seminars, and I had many conversations with him. . . .
As for many of the others, I sought them out—people like Erich Fromm
and Karen Horney and Ruth Benedict and Max Wertheimer and the like.
. . . I think it's fair to say that I have had the best teachers, both formal
and informal, of any person who ever lived, just because of the historical
accident of being in New York City when the very cream of European
intellect was migrating away from Hitler. New York City in those days
was simply fantastic. There has been nothing like it since Athens. And I
think I knew every one of them more or less well. The ones that I have
mentioned in my prefaces are the ones I felt most grateful to and knew
most closely. I cannot say that any one of them was any more important
than any other. I was just learning from everybody and from anybody

who had anything to teach me . . . I learned from all of them. . . . So I could not be said to be a Goldsteinian nor a Frommian nor an Adlerian or whatever. I never accepted any of the invitations to join any of these parochial and sectarian organizations. I learned from all of them and refused to close any doors." [3]

Among the others he mentioned as being particularly influential were Margaret Mead, Gardner Murphy, Rollo May, Carl Rogers, Kurt Goldstein, Gordon Allport—all leaders in the new science.

December 7, 1941, changed the direction of Maslow's life, as it did of so many millions of others in the world. Beyond the age of fighting, Maslow reached the decision, in those early days of World War II, to devote the rest of his life to seeking a comprehensive theory of human behavior which could be useful on a worldwide basis, a "psychology for the peace table," based on factual evidence which could be accepted by all mankind. He started working to synthesize all of the many points of view he had studied.

"I wanted to prove that human beings are capable of something grander than war and prejudice and hatred.

"I wanted to make science consider all the problems that non-scientists have been handling—religion, poetry, values, philosophy, art." [1]

Another profound influence on Maslow was his experience with the Northern Blackfoot Indian tribe in Alberta, Canada. Given a grant-in-aid by the Social Science Research Council, Maslow spent a summer with these people. His ethnological studies had already alerted him to the fact that hostility and destructiveness among primitive cultures varied in degree from 0% to 100%. And, although admittedly inadequate in scope, Dr. Maslow's findings with the Blackfoot convinced him that human aggression is the result more of culture than of heredity.

This tribe had a constant population of 800, yet Maslow could find records of only five fist fights within the last 15 years. "Intra-social hostility, for which I hunted with all the anthropological and psychiatric means at my command, was certainly at a minimum compared to our larger society." [4]

Maslow wrote that during his stay he never had a single instance of what he called cruelty or even masked aggression directed at him. He observed that children were rarely punished physically, and that the Indians looked down on white people for their cruelty toward their children and their fellow men.

Motivation and Personality was Maslow's second book. Since its publication, he has unleashed a literal flood of reports, papers, articles, speeches, and books developing, elaborating, and improving on the original presentation.

The preface to the revised edition of his *Toward a Psychology of Being* states, "Much has happened to the world of psychology since this book was first published (1962). Humanistic Psychology—that's what it's being called most frequently—is now quite solidly established as a viable, third alternative to objectivistic . . . psychology and to orthodox Freudianism. Its literature is large and is rapidly growing. Furthermore, it is beginning to be *used*, especially in education, in industry, in religion, in organization and management, in therapy, and in self-improvement and by various other 'Eupsychian' organizations, journals and individuals." [5]

"Eupsychian" is a word Maslow coined to describe human-oriented institutions, not wanting to use the overworked "Utopian," which also bears an impractical connotation. As Maslow defines it, Eupsychia refers to "the culture that would be generated by one thousand self-actualizing people on some sheltered island where they would not be interfered with . . . the word 'eupsychia' can also be taken another way. It can mean 'moving toward psychological health' . . ." [6]

Differences from Other Theories

Maslow's work is not a total rejection of Freud or of Watson and the other Behaviorists, but is rather an attempt to assess what is useful, meaningful, and applicable to mankind in both psychologies, and to go on from there.

"It is very difficult, I have found," he said, "to communicate to others my simultaneous respect for and impatience with these two comprehensive psychologies. So many people insist on being *either* pro-Freudian *or* anti-Freudian, pro-scientific *or* anti-scientific psychology, etc. In my opinion all such loyalty-positions are silly. Our job is to integrate these various truths into the *whole* truth, which should be our only loyalty." [5]

Maslow found that successful psychologists and psychiatrists were frequently forced to depart from currently popular theories in order to be successful in their work with neurotic and psychotic patients. Existing theories were not solving human problems nor did they seem adequately to explain existing facts.

Maslow was highly critical of Freud's concentration on the study of neurotic and psychotic individuals, and of the assumption that all higher forms of behavior were acquired and not natural to the human species.

It is Maslow's belief that one cannot understand mental illness until one understands mental health. Not only Freud, but Hamilton, Hobbes, and Schopenhauer, reached their conclusions about human nature by observing the worst rather than the best of man. Positive aspects of human behavior such as happiness, joy, contentment, peace of mind, satisfaction, fun, play, well-being, elation, and ecstasy have been ignored by scientists, as have such positive qualities as kindness, generosity, and friendship. Scientific emphasis has been placed on man's shortcomings, and little or no consideration has been given to his strengths and potentials.

Maslow said, "If one is preoccupied with the insane, the neurotic, the psychopath, the criminal, the delinquent, the feeble-minded, one's hopes for the human species become perforce more and more modest, more and more 'realistic', more and more scaled down, one expects less and less from people. . . . it becomes more and more clear that the study of the crippled, stunted, immature, and unhealthy specimens can yield only a cripple psychology and a cripple philosophy. The study of self-actualizing people must be the basis for a more universal science of psychology." [4]

It is this concept that makes Maslow's theory unique. He has studied the very best human beings he could find, causing him to conclude, "What is happening now is a change in the image of man. From the philosophy of human nature that people have tucked away in their bones *everything* follows. . . . In the case of the humanistic and Third Force image, which shows so clearly that we have been selling human nature short throughout the whole of recorded history, this is certainly . . . a revolution in terms of its consequences. It can and will change the world and everything in it. I feel so privileged to be at a turning point in history and to be helping with it and to know the others who make up the Third Force—Rogers, Goldstein, Allport—people like that." [7]

The Behaviorists, on the other hand, tend to study averages, placing great emphasis on statistical methods. They study what *is* rather than what could be or ought to be. Dr. Kinsey's studies of twentieth-century sexual behavior are good examples of the use of statistics to study human behavior. As Maslow points out, "It used to be normal for 75% of all babies to die before the age of five[4] . . . . We tend then to get into the situation . . . in which the normalcy from the descriptive point of view, from the value-free science point of view this normalcy or averageness is the best we can expect and that, therefore, we should be content with it."[8] The study of averages tends to lead to the concept of the "well-adjusted" person rather than the well-developed personality.

Behaviorists also base much of their research on the study of animals. Maslow finds a significant difference between human behavior and that of the animal species. Furthermore, he questions the assumption that the animal instincts are necessarily bad. His position is that even if we accept the premise that man developed from the animal and has common instincts with animals, it does not follow necessarily that these instincts are bad. Can sexual drives necessary to the perpetuation of the species be considered only as bad? Can we ignore the fact that for most of the animal kingdom there is as much good behavior as bad? Destructive aggression probably is less common among animals than it is in the human species. There are many examples of cooperation in the animal kingdom; in fact, cooperation within a species is more the rule than the exception.

Futhermore, if we assume man is merely a higher evolutionary form of animal then we must assume that his closest relative is the ape. Maslow learned from his extensive work with monkeys and apes that they are frequently loving and cooperative, rather than mean, selfish, and aggressive as Freud pictured animals. "Coordinated with the bad-animal interpretation of instincts was the expectation that they would be seen most clearly in the insane, the neurotic, the criminal, the feeble-minded, or the desperate," he said. "This follows naturally from the doctrine that conscience, rationality, and ethics are no more than an acquired veneer, completely different in character from what lies beneath."[4] . . . "Darwin was so identified with this view that he saw only competition in the animal world, completely overlooking the cooperation that is just as common."[4]

Both Freudians and Behaviorists, in emphasizing man's continuity with the animal world, tend to ignore or reject the very characteristics which make the human species uniquely different from all other animals. If various animal species have instincts unique to their species, why isn't it reasonable, Maslow asked, to assume that the human species also has unique characteristics? "The use of animals guarantees in advance the neglect of just those capacities which are uniquely human, for example, martydom, self-sacrifice, shame, love, humor, art, beauty, conscience, guilt, patriotism, ideals, the production of poetry or philosophy or music or science. Animal psychology is necessary for learning about those human characteristics that man shares with all primates. It is useless in the study of those characteristics which man does *not* share with other animals, or in which he is vastly superior, such as latent learning."[4]

Behaviorists have not only relied heavily on animals in developing their data, but they have tended to use pigeons and rats in particular. This is objectionable to Maslow because rats apparently have few instincts other than physiological ones. This approach has also led to the assumption that instincts are powerful, uncontrollable, and unmodifiable. Based on his many years of study, Maslow rejects this point of view as too narrow. "However, this may be for salmon, or frogs, or lemmings; it is not true for humans." . . .[4] Maslow said that it would be preferable to use the monkey rather than the white rat as a subject for motivation experiments simply because human beings were more like monkeys than like white rats. "The various Behaviorisms," Maslow said, "all seem to generate inexorably such a passive image of a helpless man, one who has little to say about his own fate."[9]

Nearly all American behavioral scientists since about 1920, and frequently much earlier, have adapted their study of human behavior to the "scientific" model. Their basic assumption was that the scientific approach, so tremendously successful in the solution of physical and technical problems, could be equally successful in the solution of human problems. The behavioral scientists has believed he must study man as an object—an object to be observed but not questioned. Subjective information, man's opinions about himself and his own feelings, desires, and wants, were to be ignored. Freud was so preoccupied with the unconscious determinants of human behavior that he paid little or no attention to his patients' attempts to explain their reasons for behaving as they did.

Disagreeing with this approach, Maslow was convinced that we can learn a great deal more about human nature through consideration of the subjective as well as the objective. In fact, in his experience, the subjective approach was frequently more productive; and when it was ignored, much of human behavior became meaningless. It was not that Maslow rejected science—it was that he demanded a broader approach. He feels that psychologists have been too sensitive to the opinions of physicists, chemists, and mathematicians, whose attitude is that if it cannot be reduced to an exact physical or mathematical formula it is not knowledge.

Although Maslow and other Third Force psychologists disagree with the *theories* of the Behaviorists and Freudians, they find that the *techniques* of scientific psychology and of Freud can be useful. Conditioned reflex *is* a form of learning. Free association from the Freudian couch *is* a form of communication. Said Maslow, "I believe mechanistic science (which in psychology takes the form of Behaviorism) to be not incorrect but rather too narrow and limited to serve as a general or comprehensive philosophy." [9] And of Freud he said, "Freud's picture of man was clearly unsuitable, leaving out as it did his aspirations, his realizable hopes, his godlike qualities. . . . Freud supplied to us the sick half of psychology and we must now fill it out with the healthy half." [5]

Freud and other Instinctivists tend to ignore the reality of associative learning and stimulus-response behavior, while Behaviorists tend to an overly dogmatic rejection of all instincts, good or bad. If human behavior, as the Behaviorists contend, consists almost entirely of the body's defensive removal of irritating tensions with the end product a state of passive waiting for more tensions to arise, then why do people get wiser and better? How can anyone have a zest for living, if life is merely an attempt to avoid tension? The Behaviorist, perhaps because of his emphasis on the study of animals, tends to ignore the possibility of positive motivations such as hope, joy, and optimism. As Maslow put it, "There are a considerable number of other theoretical, clinical, and experimental considerations pointing in the same direction, i.e., the desirability of re-evaluating instinct theory and perhaps even of resurrecting it in some form or other. These all support a certain skepticism with regard to the current stress by psychologists, sociologists, and anthropologists on the plasticity, flexibility, and adaptability of the human being and on his ability to learn. Human beings seem to be far more autonomous and self-governed than modern psychological theory allows for." [4]

In his book, *The Psychology of Science,* Maslow expands and elaborates on his original criticisms of physical science as a model for behavioral science. "This book," he said, "rejects the traditional but unexamined conviction that orthodox science is *the* path to knowledge or even that it is the only reliable path. I consider this conventional view to be philosophically, historically, psychologically, and sociologically naive." [9]

The Third Force Approach

The study of the mentally ill is valuable, but not enough. The study of animals is valuable, but not enough. The study of average individuals will not, in itself, solve the problem. In order to understand mental illness we need a thorough understanding of mental *health*.

Maslow proposed to introduce this important new area of information into psychology and psychiatry. He had stumbled on the idea that one could learn a great deal about man and his potential from the study of exceptionally healthy, mature people—a segment of the human species Maslow has termed the "growing tip." The details of this approach are described in the next chapter.

Maslow felt that a comprehensive theory of behavior must include the internal or intrinsic determinants of behavior as well as extrinsic or external and environmental determinants. Freud had concentrated on the first, the Behaviorists on the second. Both points of view needed to be combined. An objective study of human behavior was not enough; for complete understanding the subjective must be considered as well. We must consider peoples' feelings, desires, hopes, aspirations in order to understand their behavior.

The characteristics of behavioral scientists themselves are very important determinants of their ability to understand behavior. Dr. Maslow lists the following criteria: The scientist needs to be secure, confident, and mentally healthy in order to have a good perception of the reality he is studying. The scientist needs to approach problems with an open mind; he needs to be problem-centered rather than ego-centered. The behaviorial scientist needs a broad general knowledge; overspecialization is not productive. As Maslow points out, the greatest, most successful scientists generally have had broad interests; some of the outstanding examples are Aristotle, Einstein, Leonardo da Vinci, and Thomas Jefferson.

The successful student of human behavior needs to be more philosophical, more creative, more diverse, more intuitive, to "see reality whole," to see all the various disciplines as mutually helpful collaborators rather than separate unrelated specialties. When the emphasis is on means and methods rather than results, there tends to be a cleavage between social scientists and other truthseekers. Science should be described as the search for truth, insight, and understanding; and this search cannot be limited to those with highly specialized professional degrees. Social scientists have tried too hard to be like physical scientists, with the result that their search for new and better techniques for studying people has been limited. Orthodox science tends to put too much emphasis on instruments, techniques, procedures, apparatus, and methods rather than problems, questions, functions, or goals. Therefore, the position of technicians and "apparatus men" often becomes exaggerated, and questions, answers, and problem-solving are forgotten. Means-centered scientists tend to fit their problems to their techniques rather than the opposite. A hierarchy of sciences has been created in which physics is considered to be more "scientific" than biology, biology more "scientific" than psychology, and psychology more "scientific" than sociology. This separates the sciences and erects walls between them.

Other scientists have agreed with Maslow's demand for a broader, more comprehensive, multi-disciplinary approach to human problems. Piet Hein, the distinguished Danish scientist-philosopher said, "All problems which we try to solve lose their meaning when we amputate them, when we cut off what we want to cut off to make them fit into our random frames of specialization. You can cut so much off a problem that the rest of it has no sense. You must take the whole field of human knowledge and human activity into account in order for the problem to make sense." Another example is Jacques Loeb, who when asked whether he was a neurologist, a chemist, a physicist, a psychologist, or a philosopher, answered only, "I solve problems."

To illustrate the point that professional scientists are not the only ones qualified to solve human problems, Maslow cites the example of Synanon, an organization started by non-professionals which is achieving greater success in curing drug addicts than the professionals. Maslow describes it thus, "What we approach in the Synanon story is the ultimate absurdity of bureaucratic science, in which some portions of the truth may have to be defined as 'unscientific,' in which truth is really true only when gathered by properly certified and uniformed 'truth collectors' and according to traditionally sanctified methods or ceremonies. . . . Is the diplomat, the Ph.D., the M.D., the professional, the only person permitted to be wise?

knowledgeable? insightful? to discover? to cure? . . . is it really wise and functional to demand a college degree as a prerequisite for so many jobs rather than seeking actual education, knowledge, skill, capacity, suitability for the job?" [9]

Behavioral scientists cannot be value-free. Emphasis on "scientific techniques" encourages psychologists to be safe and sound rather than bold and daring, and convinces scientists that they are more objective than they actually are. Their conclusions become ethically neutral. Such scientists avoid the important questions of ethics, morals, right and wrong, healthy and unhealthy behavior—questions to which our society needs to know the answers. By becoming overly pragmatic, psychology avoids important areas such as pleasure, fun, play, beauty, art, joy, love, and happiness. Maslow finds that moral and spiritual problems fall within the realm of nature and considers them part of science, not an opposing realm. He says that science, in its role as a social institution and as a human enterprise, does have goals, ethics, morals, purposes—or, in simplest terms, values.

The search for exact "scientific" answers in the study of human behavior can be unhealthy—there are too many areas where scientific research is weak or nonexistent. In the absence of exact knowledge we must use whatever knowledge is available. "Knowledge," Maslow says, "is a matter of degree. Any increment of knowledge or of reliability is better than doing nothing. . . . There are some who will insist that 'scientific' knowledge is and must be clear, lucid, unequivocally defined, unmistakable, demonstrable, repeatable, communicable, logical, rational, verbalizable, conscious. If it is not these, then it is not 'scientific'; it is something else. But what shall we say, then, about the first stages of knowledge, the precursor of these final forms, the beginnings that each of us can easily enough experience in himself? [9] It is both useful and correct to consider as falling within the definition of knowledge all "protoknowledge,' so long as its probability of being correct is greater than chance . . . knowledge is then seen as more reliable or less reliable but still knowledge so long as its probability is greater than chance." [9]

Maslow is also critical of what he calls the atomistic approach; the approach, common in physical science, of breaking things down into their component parts and studying the component parts separately. Man, he believes, must be studied as an entity, as a system. Each part is related to the other part, and, unless you study them all as a whole, the answers are incomplete. Most behavioral scientists have attempted to isolate independent drives, urges, and instincts, and study them separately. This Maslow found to be generally less productive than the holistic approach which holds that the whole is more than the sum of its parts.

CHAPTER 3

The Study of
Self-actualization

Maslow's study of outstanding examples of mental health started, not as a scientific research project, but as an effort to satisfy his personal curiosity. He had not expected such exciting implications from the study. The results were important, even though the study fell short of scientific methodological requirements. As Dr. Maslow says, "The problem of mental health and illness is so urgent that any bits of information are helpful. If we were to wait for conventionally reliable data, we should have to wait forever." [1]

The investigation of self-actualized people resulted from Maslow's curiosity when a student. He was trying to understand two professors whom he respected and admired very much. They were Maslow's teachers after he had received his Ph.D. and had come to New York City. His curiosity compelled him to analyze what it was about these two educators that made them so different, so outstanding. As he made notes about them it suddenly struck him that the two personalities could be compared, that there were certain characteristics which were common to both of these people. Excited by this discovery, young Maslow sought to discover whether this type of individual could be found in other places. From this search came his more extensive studies of fully mature people.

The individuals he studied were selected from his personal acquaintances and friends, from public figures, living and dead, and selected college students. In the first attempt with young people, two thousand college students were considered, but only one sufficiently mature individual was found. It was decided later to choose the healthiest 1% of the Brandeis College population.

The definition of the self-actualized person was still vague, but Maslow loosely described it as "the full use and exploitation of talent, capacities, potentialities-etc. Such people seem to be fulfilling themselves and doing the best that they are capable of doing." [1] The negative criterion was an absence of tendencies toward psychological problems, neurosis, or psychosis. The self-actualized person was the best possible specimen of the human species, a representative of what Maslow later came to call the "growing tip."

This approach was a rejection of the customary statistical approach used in behavioral science which takes the average of the species. The example he used was: If you wanted to know how fast a man could run a mile or how to improve your ability to run a mile, you didn't study the average runner, you studied the exceptional runner, those at the growing tip. Only those individuals will give you an idea of man's potential to run a better mile. However, he found he could not exclude individuals on the basis of single errors, mistakes, or bad habits. In other words, he could not use perfection as a basis for selection because none of his subjects was perfect.

One of the problems encountered was that in all cases it was almost impossible to get the full information generally demanded in clinical work. Possible subjects became self-conscious, froze, laughed off the effort, or broke off the relationship. As a result of this early experience Maslow found that all older subjects had to be studied indirectly or almost surreptitiously. He found that only young people could be studied directly.

Inasmuch as living people, whose names could not be mentioned, were studied, two requirements of ordinary scientific work became impossible: repeatability of the investigation and public availability of the data from which the conclusions were drawn. This was partially overcome by the use of public and historical figures, and by supplementary study of young people and children, who could be used publicly.

He divided his study into three categories of "cases, partial cases, and potential or possible cases." Included in the first category were Abraham Lincoln, Thomas Jefferson, Albert Einstein, Eleanor Roosevelt, Jane Addams, William James, Spinoza, Albert Schweitzer, and Aldous Huxley. The "partial cases" category included five contemporaries who fall short but can still be used for study. In the potential or possible cases were included twenty younger people who seemed to be developing in the direction of self-actualization and such people as G.W. Carver, Eugene V. Debs, Thomas Eakins, Fritz Kreisler, Goethe, Pablo Casals, Martin Buber, Danilo Dolci, Arthur E. Morgan, John Keats, David Hilbert, Arthur Waley, D.T. Susuki, Adlai Stevenson, Sholom Aleichem, Robert Browning, Ralph Waldo Emerson, Frederick Douglass, Joseph Schumpeter, Robert Benchley, Ida Tarbell, Harriet Tubman, George Washington, Karl Muenzinger, Joseph Hayden, Camille Pissaro, Edward Bibring, George William Russell, Pierre Renoir, Henry Wadsworth Longfellow, Peter Kropotkin, John Altgeld, Thomas More, Edward Bellamy, Benjamin Franklin, John Muir, Walt Whitman. The study of these individuals, their habits, their characteristics, their personalities, their abilities led Maslow to his definition of mental health and his theory of human motivation. The method opens a whole new area to behavioral science. "It may now become feasible," said Maslow, "through the study of self-fulfilling individuals, to have our eyes open to all sorts of basic insights, old to the philosophers but new to us." [2]

Characteristics of Self-actualization

Maslow first called the exceptional people he studied "self-actualized" people. Self-actualization, he said, "is only in older people, tends to be seen as an ultimate or final state of affairs, a far goal, rather than a dynamic process active throughout life, Being rather than Becoming." [2]

As "self-actualized" people are usually sixty years of age or more, most people do not belong in this category; they are not static, they have not arrived; but they are moving toward maturity. The actualization process means the development or discovery of the true self and the development of existing or latent potential. In later publications Maslow suggests that perhaps a more descriptive word is "fully human." Not all highly productive, successful, talented people meet the description of psychological health, maturity, or self-actualization. Some very famous people were not psychologically healthy—Byron, Van Gogh, and Wagner, among others. From the study of exceptional people a number of characteristics began to crystallize regarding the aspects of mental health. On the following pages some of the common characteristics of superior specimens of the human species will be described.

Probably the most universal and common aspect of these superior people is their ability to see life clearly, to see it as it is rather than as they wish it to be. They are less emotional and more objective about their observations. Most people hear what they want to hear from other people, even when it is not entirely true or sincere but self-actualizing people do not allow their hopes and wishes to distort their observations. They are far above average in their ability to judge people correctly and to see through the phony or the fake. Generally speaking, their choice of marriage partners is far better than average, although by no means perfect.

Because of their superior perception, the self-actualizing are more decisive and have a clearer notion of what is right and wrong. They are more accurate in their prediction of future events. This ability of these "fully human" persons to see more efficiently, to be better in their judgment, extends to many areas of life, involving the understanding not only of people but of art, music, politics, and philosophy. Self-actualizing people penetrate and see concealed and confused realities more swiftly and accurately than average individuals.

Yet, they have a kind of humility, the ability to listen carefully to others, to admit that they don't know everything and that other people can teach them something. In part, this superior perception results from and in a better understanding of self. This concept can also be described as a child-like simplicity and lack of arrogance—children frequently have this ability to hear without preconception or early judgment. "As the child looks out upon the world with wide, uncritical, innocent eyes, simply noting or observing what is the case, without either arguing the matter or demanding that it be otherwise, so does the self-actualizing person look upon human nature in himself and in others." [1]

The self-actualized person's perception is less distorted by desires, anxieties, fears, hopes, false optimism, or pessimism. Maslow termed this non-judgmental type of perception, "Being cognition" or "B-cognition." It is a passive and receptive type of observation. He also calls it "desireless awareness." Being-cognition alone is not enough. As Maslow points out, it can lead to too great a tolerance, too much indiscriminate acceptance, and loss of taste. Therefore, these full-mature individuals perceive in two ways: contemplatively (Being-cognition) and decisively. When cognition shifts to the second kind of perception, decision, judgment, condemnation, planning, and action become possible.

Without exception, he found self-actualizing people to be dedicated to some work, task, duty, or vocation which they considered important. Because they were interested in this work, they worked hard, yet the usual distinction between work and play became blurred. For them work was exciting and pleasurable. It seems that commitment to an important job is a major requirement for growth, self-actualization, and happiness. However, it is not enough to have an important job—the self-actualizing person must be doing it well. If he is a physician, he must be a good physician, not a poor one. This involves hard work, discipline, training, and often postponement of pleasure.

Maslow found creativity to be a universal characteristic of all the self-actualizing people he studied. Creativeness was almost synonymous with health, self-actualization, and full humanness. Characteristics associated with this creativity were flexibility, spontaneity, courage, willingness to make mistakes, openness, and humility. As mentioned, in many respects the creativity of these people is similar to that of children before they have learned to fear the ridicule of others, while they are still able to see things freshly and without prejudgment. Maslow believes this to be a characteristic which is too frequently lost as people grow older. Self-actualizing people either do not lose this fresh, naive approach or, if they lose it, they recover it later in life. "Almost any child," says Maslow, "can compose a song or poem or a dance or a painting or a play or a game on the spur of the moment, without planning or previous intent." [2]

Spontaneity, also, is almost synonymous with creativity. Self-actualizing people are less inhibited; and therefore, more expressive, natural, and simple. They do not usually feel it necessary to mask their feelings or thoughts or play artificial roles. Creativity requires courage, the ability for one to stick one's neck out, to be able to ignore criticism and ridicule; and the ability to resist the influence of one's culture. "Every one of our great creators . . . has testified to the element of courage that is needed in the lonely moment of creation, affirming something new (contradictory to the old). This is a kind of daring, a going out in front all alone, a defiance, a challenge. The moment of fright is quite understandable, but must nevertheless be overcome if creation is to be possible." [3] Thus, while these individuals are humble in the sense that they are open to new ideas and quick to admit ignorance and error, they are also arrogant in the sense that they are willing to forego popularity in order to stand up for a new idea. In part, this comes from their ability to concentrate on the job to be done and to forget themselves. They are self-confident and have self-respect; because of this they are more concerned with the job to be done than with protecting their egos.

Because of their courage, their lack of fear, they are willing to make silly mistakes. The truly creative person is one who can think "crazy"; such a person knows full well that many of his great ideas will prove to be worthless. The creative person is flexible—he is able to change as the situation changes, to break habits, to face indecision and changes in conditions without undue stress. He is not threatened by the unexpected as rigid, inflexible people are.

Maslow assumes that most people have far more creativity than they are utilizing. He does not reject that genius may have a genetic basis. There is very little research about this, but there is some indication that great talent may be inherited as well as acquired. However, Maslow points out that the great person is also a hard worker. "Inspirations are a dime a dozen. The difference between the inspiration and the final product, for example, Tolstoy's *War and Peace,* is an awful lot of hard work, an awful lot of discipline, an awful lot of training. . . . the virtues which go with the secondary kind of creativeness, the creativeness which results in the actual products, in the great paintings, the great novels, in the bridges, the new inventions, and so on, rest as heavily upon other virtues—stubbornness and patience and hard work and so on, as they do upon the creativeness of the personality." [4]

A characteristic of the self-actualized person is the low degree of self-conflict. He is not at war with himself; his personality is integrated. This means that he has more energy for productive purposes. "Trust, goodness and beauty are in the average person in our culture only fairly well corre-

lated with each other, and in the neurotic person even less so. It is only in
the evolved and mature human being, in the self-actualizing, fully-
functioning person that they are so highly correlated that for all practical
purposes they may be said to fuse into a unity." [2]

This discovery, Dr. Maslow points out, is in direct contradiction to a
basic axiom guiding nearly all modern scientific thought—the axiom that
the more objective, factual, and scientific perception becomes, the more
removed it is from morality or values. Modern intellectuals have come to
believe that facts and values are in contradiction with each other; that
they are mutually exclusive. The study of superior individuals, Dr. Maslow
believes, refutes this cornerstone of modern "scientific" faith. There is a
scientific basis for determining right and wrong behavior, since what the
psychologically healthy person wants is identical to what is usually considered right and reasonable. For this reason, these people waste little
time or energy protecting themselves from themselves. They are not afraid
of their own desires; their impulses are in accord with reason. "Their appe-
tites agree with their judgments." [1]

Pitirim Sorokin, Harvard researcher, found that what is true is also good
and beautiful. Maslow says that his research confirms Sorokin, "provided
that we are talking only about healthy people." The healthy individual has
less confusion about what is right or wrong, good or bad, and has little
trouble operating on his perception of right behavior. Contrary to the assumption of many scientists and theologians, Maslow finds that the psychologically healthy person is both selfish and unselfish; in fact, these two
attitudes merge into one. The healthy person finds happiness in helping
others. Thus, for him unselfishness is selfish. "They get selfish pleasures
from the pleaures of other people, which is a way of saying unselfish." [5]
The healthy person is selfish in a healthy way, a way which is beneficial to
him and to society, too.

Related to this selfish-unselfish attitude is the previously mentioned attitude of the healthy individual toward work and play. He enjoys play; he
enjoys work; his work becomes play; his vocation and avocation become
the same. The research indicates that healthy people are most integrated
when facing a great creative challange, some worthwhile goal, or a serious
threat or emergency. The self-actualizing person not only has a more harmonious personality, but he sees the world in a more unified way. As he
becomes more unified as an individual he sees more unity, and possibility

for unity, in the world. It is this type of perception which enables the great inventor to produce something new and different from elements which had been considered unrelated to each other.

In these mature individuals the struggle between good and bad is not a problem. They consistently choose and prefer the better values, and it is easy for them to do so. This dichotomy between good and bad is present only in the average individual who is not consistent with himself. As an example Maslow points out that there is a great deal of scientific data now available to indicate that it is psychologically desirable for children to be accepted, protected, loved, and respected, and this is precisely what children instinctively desire. That merging of desires is now often referred to as the process of synergy.

The mature individual has a healthy respect for himself, a respect based upon knowledge that he is competent and adequate. Although he is not dependent upon it, he frequently receives deserved respect from others. Such a person does not need or value unwarranted fame or notoriety. He has a feeling of power in the sense that he has a feeling of self control. He is in control of himself and his destiny; he is not afraid of himself, ashamed of himself, or discouraged by his mistakes. It is not that he is perfect; he makes mistakes too, but he takes them in stride.

The psychologically healthy individual is highly independent, yet at the same time enjoys people. He has a healthy desire for privacy which is quite different from the neurotic, secretive, fearful privacy of the poorly adjusted. They are sometimes seen by others as being remote and detached because, while they enjoy the company of others, they do not need other people. They rely fully upon their own capacities. Frequently their abilities are so superior they actually feel hampered by others. They are both the most individualistic members of society, and, at the same time, the most social, friendly, and loving. They are governed far more by inner directives, their own nature, and natural needs than by the society or the environment. "Since they depend less on other people, they are less ambivalent about them, less anxious and also less hostile, less needful of their praise and their affection. They are less anxious for honors, prestige, and rewards." [2]

Self-actualizers have what Maslow calls "psychological freedom." They are able to make their own decisions even in the face of contrary popular opinion. They resist their culture when it does not agree with their own point of view. They are not generally unconventional about things which they do not consider important: language, clothes, food, etc.; yet they can become extremely independent and unconventional when they feel basic principles are involved.

Only one of the subjects studied by Maslow was religious in the orthodox sense of the word. Yet all of them, with the exception of one who was an acknowledged atheist, had a belief in a meaningful universe and a life which could be called spiritual. Nearly all had clear ideas of right and wrong based upon their own experience rather than blind acceptance of religious revelation. In spite of this fact, the characteristics of self-actualized people are similar in many respects to the values and ideals taught by the great religions . . . "e.g., the transcendence of self, the fusion of the true, the good and the beautiful, contribution to others, wisdom, honesty, and naturalness, the transcendence of selfish and personal motivations, the giving up of 'lower' desires in favor of 'higher' ones, . . . the decrease of hostility, cruelty, and destructiveness and the increase of friendliness, kindness, etc." [2]

For these individuals self-discipline is relatively easy because what they desire to do agrees with what they believe is right. Their values are based on what is real for them, rather than what others tell them. "They live within a system of stable values and not in a robot world of no values at all . . ." [1] They are responsible because they believe responsibility is rewarding.

The average individual is motivated by deficiencies—he is seeking to fulfill his basic needs for safety, belongingness, love, respect, and self esteem. The healthy man is "primarily motivated by his need to develop and actualize his fullest potentialities and capacities." [1] The healthy individual, in other words, is motivated primarily by a desire for self-actualization. Dr. Maslow believes that the term motivation does not correctly apply to most mature individuals. They are spontaneous; they are doing what is natural; they are merely expressing themselves. Scientific psychologists, says Dr. Maslow, have almost completely ignored fun and pleasure, aimless, casual, and random behavior. He attributes this to the widely accepted scientific dogma that all behavior is motivated. He challenges this axiom, stating that expressive behavior "is either unmotivated or, anyway, less motivated than coping behavior . . ." [2] In a later statement he has called this impulse to act beyond the basic needs, meta-motivation.

The self-actualizing people of the type Maslow studied are a tiny percentage of the total population, a fraction of one percent. They are very different from the average person, and few really understand them. Yet these superior people have a deep feeling of kinship with the whole human race. They are capable of sharing a type of friendship with people of suitable character, regardless of their race, creed, class, education, political beliefs, or color. This acceptance of others cuts right across political, economic, and national boundaries.

They tend to form deep, close personal friendships, deeper than those of the average adult. Generally, those with whom they associate are also healthier and more mature than average. While their interpersonal ties are deep, they are generally with only a few individuals. Their circle of intimate friends is usually small. Because they are superior in character, capacity, and talent they tend to associate closely with others of similar capacity. It is not unusual for them to attract admirers, friends, and "disciples," and when this happens the relationship between the self-actualizing person and his admirers is rather one-sided. These healthy individuals can be very tolerant of other's shortcomings, and yet they are very intolerant about dishonesty, lying, cheating, cruelty, and hypocrisy. When real crimes are involved, righteous indignation is an almost universal characteristic of the self-actualizing person.

These people, says Maslow, contradict two common aphorisms: opposites attract, and like marries like. These healthy individuals tend to seek people with similar character traits, such as honesty, sincerity, kindliness, and courage, but disregard superficial characteristics such as class, education, religion, national background, and appearance. In this respect, the healthy individuals are not threatened by differences. "As a consequence, it is easily possible for self-actualizing people to fall deeply in love with homely partners. . . . The more mature they become, the less attracted they are by such characteristics as handsome, good looking, good dancer, nice breasts, physically strong, tall, handsome body, good necker, and the more they speak of compatibility, goodness, decency, good companionship, considerateness." [1]

These healthy individuals are not without problems. However, generally their pains and problems are fewer, and they enjoy happiness and pleasure more. They are not universally calm; temper outbursts are not unusual. They may be easily bored by idle gossip, gay conversation, and the typical cocktail-party situation. They, too, suffer moments of guilt, anxiety, sadness, and self-doubt. They have a sense of humor, but not of the ordinary type; they do not laugh at humor which ridicules people or makes someone else appear inferior. They prefer a philosophical or cosmic humor. Lincoln's humor serves as a perfect example.

The relationships that fully mature people develop are better for themselves and for others. Whether it be a friendship relationship, a marriage relationship, or a parent-child relationship, it is never exploitative. The healthy individual, because he has great respect for himself, is able to be more respectful to others. This is supported by Erich Fromm's contention that true self-love or self-respect is harmonious with, rather than antagonistic to, love for others. The average individual, lacking sufficient self-respect, does not form deep respectful relationships with others. "The love that is found in healthy people," says Maslow, "is much better described in terms of spontaneous admiration and the kind of receptive and understanding awe and enjoyment that we experience when struck by a fine painting." [1] These people need less love from others and are able to remain alone for long periods, but at the same time they are able to give love—they are more loving people.

Generally speaking, the psychologically healthy individual seems more likely to form a strong, happy, lasting marriage. It is not a selfless marriage, but rather a healthily selfish marriage in which each partner enjoys the other and the other's success. Although they take great pleasure in each other's company, they are capable of standing long separation or death philosophically. Each partner in a healthy marriage increases the confidence and self respect of the other, they are good for each other. Maslow's data contradicts the age-old theory of basic hostility between the sexes—this condition does not exist in a healthy marriage. If one of the partners is bad, however, increasing familiarity will not strengthen the marriage, but will weaken it. A good marriage becomes stronger with time.

Not only do the partners enjoy each other more with time, but their sexual life also improves with age—up to a point, at least. They enjoy sex more, as they do all life activities, and yet they can do without it when necessary. They seldom seek sex alone, for them sex includes a loving relationship. They seldom seek love affairs outside of marriage, and yet they are attracted to the opposite sex and find it easy to enjoy friendship with the opposite sex without fear.

Maslow remarked that Dr. Kinsey, in his survey of sexual behavior, confused average with normal. The study of self-actualizing people and their sexual relationships indicates that perhaps what is average is not normal or healthy.

The superior person sometimes finds it desirable to be constructively critical. Usually people criticize in anger, but Maslow finds that under some circumstances the loving person feels it is right to call the friend or marriage partner's attention to some consistent error of which they may not be aware—a reverse of the old saw, "even your best friends won't tell you." He cites the Bruderhof, the Christian sect which considers it an aspect of Christian love to be honest with one another, to be honest even if it may hurt at the moment. The Bruderhof consider it unloving to let someone go on making the same mistake again and again just because others don't have the courage to tell him.

Based on his study of these superior human beings, Maslow asks the question: why can there not be a technology of joy, of happiness? His study showed that Plato and Socrates were right in their contention that virtue is rewarding. He found that self-actualizing people enjoy life more —not that they don't have pain, sorrow, and troubles, just that they get more out of life. They appreciate it more; they have more interests; they are more aware of beauty in the world. They have less fear and anxiety, and more confidence and relaxation. They are far less bothered by feelings of boredom, despair, shame, or lack of purpose. "They spontaneously tend to do right, because that is what they *want* to do, what they *need* to do, what they enjoy, what they approve of doing, and what they will continue to enjoy. It is this unity, this network of positive intercorrelation that falls apart into separateness and conflict as the person gets psychologically sick." [6]

Or to put it another way, "self-actualizing people enjoy life in general and in practically all its aspects, while most other people enjoy only stray moments of triumph, of achievement or of climax or peak experience." [2] They never tire of life. They have the capacity to appreciate the sunrise or sunset or marriage or nature again and again.

The healthy individual shows far less fear than the average adult who is less influenced by truth, logic, justice, reality, and beauty. These healthy individuals are not often threatened by the external situation as they have great confidence in their ability to handle whatever confronts them. They are almost uniformly unthreatened by the unknown and the mysterious. In fact, they are usually attracted to the unknown. This is in sharp contrast with the neurotic person's fear of the unfamiliar and the mysterious. Maslow quotes Albert Einstein as being typical of this fearless attitude: "The most beautiful thing we can experience is the mysterious. It is the source of all art and science." [1] Not only is the self-actualizing person less afraid of his environment, he is also less afraid of himself. He accepts himself and his nature philosophically, in fact, he gives it far less consideration than the neurotic person.

Maslow found that the outstanding people he studied had a number of other common characteristics. They had the ability to be objective and problem-centered, which involves a certain personal detachment from the problem. However, the same detachment in social relationships occasionally causes trouble because it can be interpreted as coldness, aloofness, snobbishness, even hostility. They have an unusual ability to concentrate, and this sometimes produces absent-mindedness. Because they have fewer problems of their own, they tend to be working to solve problems of society; they have some mission in life. They are more concerned with ends rather than means.

They are usually friendly and interested in children and good with them. However, they do not always make good parents because they are so competent that it is sometimes discouraging to their own children. In general they tend to be kind or, at least, patient with most other people. "They have for human beings in general a deep feeling of identification, sympathy and affection in spite of the occasional anger, impatience, or disgust . . . they have a genuine desire to help the human race." [1]

They are sufficiently philosophical to be patient and seek or accept slow orderly change, rather than sudden change. While the average adult in our society tends to be either highly practical or highly theoretical, the self-actualizing person is more apt to be both theoretical and practical. He likes happy endings; he wants to see virtue rewarded and cruelty, exploitation, and evil penalized. He enjoys doing good things and punishing evil, and takes pleasure in rewarding, praising, and recognizing the talents of others. He has enough self-respect, he does not need love from everyone, and he is willing to make enemies if necessary. He also enjoys calm, peace, quiet, and relaxation. He likes to be efficient and effective, and dislikes inefficiency. He manages to love the world as it is, while seeing its defects and working to improve them. His excellent perception of reality enables him to see both the good and evil in each situation, and he enjoys solving problems and bringing order out of chaos. He is seldom mean or petty or inconsiderate of others; he appreciates the fine qualities in others and is able to ignore their faults. He enjoys his work and strives to be more efficient, better, neater, simpler, and faster.

The study of self-actualizing people refutes the Freudian theory that the human unconscious (id) is only bad, evil, crazy, or dangerous. In self-actualizing people, the subconscious is creative, loving, positive, and healthy.

CHAPTER 4

The Theory of
Basic Needs

Abraham Maslow's theory of human motivation can be applied to almost every aspect of individual and social life. He considered the following assumptions necessary for a sound theory of motivation:

The individual is an integrated, organized whole. "It is unusal, not usual," he says, "that an act or a conscious wish have but one motivation." [1] In other words the *whole* person is motivated, not just a part of him. When a man is hungry he's hungry all over; he himself wants food, not just his stomach.

Most desires and drives in the individual are interrelated. This may not be true for some of the more fundamental needs such as hunger, but it is certainly true for the more complex needs such as love.

Most previous studies have assumed that needs can be isolated and studied individually, in terms of means and ends. A full understanding of motivation requires emphasis on the fundamental end or objective rather than the means taken to reach it. When studied on a broad, cross-cultural basis, ends are far more universal than the various methods taken to achieve them. That is, while the methods vary greatly among races and cultures, the ultimate ends seem to be identical.

The human being is motivated by a number of basic needs which are species-wide, apparently unchanging, and genetic or instinctual in origin. This is a unique fundamental concept of Maslow's theoretical point of view. The needs are also psychological rather than purely physiological. They are the true inner nature of the human species, but they are weak, easily distorted, and overcome by incorrect learning, habit, or tradition. "They are," states Maslow, "intrinsic aspects of human nature which culture cannot kill, but only repress." [2] This obviously challenges an ancient and persistent belief, held by many, that instincts are strong, unchangeable, and bad. Maslow suggests the contrary: The needs are easily ignored or suppressed and are "not bad but either neutral or good." [1]

A characteristic may be considered a basic need if it meets the following conditions:

"1. Its absence breeds illness.

2. Its presence prevents illness.

3. Its restoration cures illness.

4. Under certain, very complex, free-choice situations, it is preferred by the deprived person over other satisfactions.

5. It is found to be inactive, at a low ebb, or functionally absent in the healthy person." [3]

Physiological Needs

The most basic, the most powerful, the most obvious of all man's needs are his needs for physical survival: his needs for food, liquid, shelter, sex, sleep and oxygen. A person who is lacking food, self-esteem, and love will demand food first and, until this need is satisfied, will ignore or push all other needs into the background. "For the man who is extremely and dangerously hungry, no other interests exist but food. He dreams food, he remembers food, he thinks about food, he emotes only about food, he perceives only food, and he wants only food. . . . Such a man can fairly be said to live by bread alone." [1]

Maslow says that it would be possible, but probably not very helpful, to make a long list of physiological needs, depending on how specific one wanted to get. One could probably demonstrate, for example, how various sensory pleasures such as tastes, smells, stroking, etc., could be included among the physiological needs affecting behavior. Further, while the physiological needs can be separated and identified more easily than the higher needs, they cannot be treated as separate, isolated phenomena. For instance, a person who thinks he is hungry may actually be feeling a lack of love or security or some other need. Conversely, some people satisfy, or attempt to satisfy, hunger needs by other activities such as smoking or drinking water. Thus, all human needs are interrelated.

Physiological needs have been recognized and emphasized by the two other major schools of psychology. The Behaviorists have contended that man's only genetic drives are physiological. Maslow remarks that this might stem from the fact that much Behavioristic research has been done with rats, and rats apparently have few motivations other than physiological.

Maslow thinks that the Behaviorists are correct in identifying physiological needs as having powerful influences on man's behavior, but only as long as they are unfulfilled. However, for many individuals in civilized society these lower needs are fairly well-satisfied. "But what happens to man's desires when there is plenty of bread and when his belly is full?" Maslow asks, then answers, "At once other (and higher) needs emerge, and these, rather than physiological hungers, dominate the organism. And when these in turn are satisfied, again new (and still higher) needs emerge, and so on. This is what we mean by saying that the basic human needs are organized into a hierarchy of relative prepotency." [1] Maslow contends that throughout his life the human being is practically always desiring something, he is a wanting animal and "rarely reaches a state of complete satisfaction except for a short time. As one desire is satisfied, another pops up to take its place." [1]

The Safety Needs

Once the physiological needs are sufficiently satisfied, what Maslow describes as safety needs emerge. Since the safety needs are generally satisfied in the healthy, normal adult, they can be understood best by observing children or neurotic adults. Child psychologists and teachers have found that children need a predictable world; a child prefers consistency, fairness and a certain amount of routine. When these elements are absent he becomes anxious and insecure. Freedom within limits rather than total permissiveness is preferred; in fact, it is necessary for the development of well-adjusted children, according to Maslow.

Insecure or neurotic adults behave much like insecure children. "Such a person," says Maslow, "behaves as if a great catastrophe were almost always impending, i.e., he is usually responding as if to an emergency . . . that is to say, a neurotic adult may be said to behave as if he were actually afraid of a spanking . . ." [1] The insecure person has a compulsive need for order and stability and goes to great lengths to avoid the strange and the unexpected. The healthy person also seeks order and stability, but it is not the life or death necessity that it is for the neurotic. The mature individual also has an interest in the new and the mysterious.

The Belongingness and Love Needs

When the physiological and safety needs are met, needs for love, affection, and belongingness emerge. "Now the person. . ." Maslow states, "will hunger for affectionate relations with people in general, namely, for a place in his group, and he will strive with great intensity to achieve this goal. He will want to attain such a place more than anything else in the world and maybe even forget that once, when he was hungry, he sneered at love as unreal or unnecessary or unimportant." [1]

Love, as Maslow uses the word, is not to be confused with sex, which can be studied as a purely physiological need. He says, "Ordinarily, sexual behavior is multidetermined . . . not only by sexual but by other needs, chief among which are the love and affection needs." [1] He likes Carl Rogers' definition of love as "that of being deeply understood and deeply accepted."

His contention is that the Freudian tendency to derive love from sex is a bad mistake. "Of course Freud is not alone in this error, . . . it is shared by many less thoughtful citizens—but he may be taken as its most influential exponent in western civilization . . . the most widely accepted of the various theories put forth by Freud is that tenderness is aim-inhibited sexuality." [1]

Maslow found that psychology had amazingly little to say about love.

"One might reasonably expect that the writers of serious treatises on the family, on marriage, and on sex should consider the subject of love to be a proper, even basic, part of their self-imposed task. But I must report that no single one of the volumes on these subjects available in the library where I work has any serious mention of the subject. More often, the word love is not even indexed." [1]

And yet, Maslow found that the absence of love stifles growth and the development of potential. Clinicians have found repeatedly that babies require love. Many other students of psychopathology have considered the thwarting of love needs as a prime cause of maladjustment. "Love hunger is a deficiency disease," Maslow states, "like salt hunger or the avitaminoses . . . It would not occur to anyone to question the statement that we 'need' iodine or vitamin C. I remind you that the evidence that we 'need' love is of exactly the same type." [3]

Love, to Maslow, involves a healthy, loving relationship between two people, which includes mutual trust. In the proper relationship, there is a lack of fear, a dropping of defenses. Love is frequently impaired when one of the partners is afraid that his weaknesses and faults will be discovered. Karl Menninger describes this problem: "Love is impaired less by the feeling that we are not appreciated than by a dread, more or less felt by everyone, lest others see through our masks, the masks of repression that have been forced upon us by convention and culture. It is this that leads us to shun intimacy, to maintain friendships on a superficial level, to underestimate and fail to appreciate others lest they come to appreciate us too well." [1]

Maslow says, "The love needs involve both giving *and* receiving love. . . . We *must* understand love; we must be able to teach it, to create it, to predict it, or else the world is lost to hostility and suspicion." [1]

The Esteem Needs

Maslow found that people have two categories of esteem needs—self-respect and esteem from other people. 1. Self-esteem includes such needs as desire for confidence, competence, mastery, adequacy, achievement, independence, and freedom. 2. Respect from others includes such concepts as prestige, recognition, acceptance, attention, status, reputation, and appreciation. Esteem needs were generally ignored by Sigmund Freud, but were stressed by Alfred Adler. A person who has adequate self-esteem is more confident and capable and, thus, more productive. However, when the self-esteem is inadequate the individual has feelings of inferiority and helplessness, which may result in discouragement and possible neurotic behavior. "The most stable and, therefore, the most healthy self-esteem is based on *deserved* respect from others rather than on external fame or celebrity and unwarranted adulation." [1]

Maslow theorizes that freedom may be a basic psychological need but points out that scientific data to support this position is far from adequate. "We may assume on the basis of commonly known clincial data that a man who has known true freedom (not paid for by giving up safety and security, but rather built on the basis of adequate safety and security) will not willingly or easily allow his freedom to be taken away from him. But we do not know if this is true for the person born into slavery." [1]

The Self-actualization Needs

"What a man *can* be, he *must* be." [1] The identification of the psychological need for growth, development, and utilization of potential—what Maslow calls self-actualization—is an important aspect of his theory of human motivation. Maslow has also described this need as "the desire to become more and more what one is, to become everything that one is capable of becoming." [1] Maslow finds that the need for self-actualization generally emerges after a reasonable satisfaction of the love and esteem needs.

The Desire to Know and to Understand

Maslow believes that a characteristic of mental health is curiosity. Admittedly, scientific and clincial data clearly establishing this as a basic need are not adequate, and a study of the subject is missing in the work of the early theorists: Freud, Adler, and Jung. Maslow lists the following reasons for advancing curiosity as a species-wide characteristic. 1. Curiosity is frequently observed in the behavior of animals. 2. History supplies many examples of men seeking knowledge even in the face of great danger; Galileo and Columbus, for example. 3. Studies of psychologically-mature individuals show that they are attracted to the mysterious, the unknown, and the unexplained. 4. Maslow's clinical experience offers cases in which previously healthy adults suffered boredom, loss of interest in life, depression, and self-dislike. Such symptoms can be produced by intelligent people "leading stupid lives in stupid jobs . . . I have seen *many* women, intelligent, prosperous, and unoccupied, slowly develop these symptoms of intellectual inanimation. Those who followed the recommendation to immerse themselves in something worthy of them showed improvement or cure often enough to impress me with the reality of the cognitive needs." [1] 5. Children seem to be naturally curious. 6. The satisfaction of curiosity is subjectively satisfying; individuals report that learning and discovery produce satisfaction and happiness.

Many behavioral scientists contend that the search for order, system, and stability is a form of compulsive neurosis. Maslow contends that, while this is true, the same characteristic behavior, lacking the obsessive quality, is found in healthy, mature individuals. In Maslow's words, "This process has been phrased by some as the search for meaning. We shall then postulate a desire to understand, to systematize, to organize, to analyze, to look for relations and meanings, to construct a system of values." [1]

The Aesthetic Needs

Behavioral science has generally ignored the possibility that people have an instinctual, or instinctoid, need for beauty. Maslow found that, at least in some individuals, the need for beauty was very deep, and ugliness was actually sickening to them. This was confirmed in some of his early studies with students concerning the effects of beautiful or ugly surroundings on them. The experiments showed that the effects of ugliness were dulling and stultifying. Dr. Maslow found that—in the strictest biological terms, in the same realm of discourse as the need for calcium in the diet—one *needs* beauty; beauty helps one to be healthier.

He pointed out that aesthetic needs are related to one's self-image. Those who are not made healthier by beauty are limited by low images of themselves. A sloppy person is ill at ease in a spotless fancy restaurant because he feels he doesn't "deserve" it.

He told the poignant story of a patient of one of his psychiatrist friends. The man had always downgraded himself, having a very, very low sense of worth. He felt he was not worth keeping alive. When he finally did commit suicide, he chose to shoot himself on top of a garbage dump; such was his opinion of himself. This was the case of a man who didn't believe he "deserved" beauty.

Maslow also observed that the need for beauty is almost universally present in healthy children. He contends that evidence of these impulses toward aesthetic needs is found in every culture and in every age as far back as the caveman.

Pre-conditions for Basic Need Satisfaction

Closely related to individual motivation are the environmental or social conditions in the society. Among the conditions prerequisite to basic need satisfaction, Maslow lists such conditions as freedom to speak, freedom to do what one wishes as long as no harm is done to others, freedom of inquiry, freedom to defend oneself, justice, honesty, fairness, and order. Threats to these preconditions evoke a reaction from the individual similar to that evoked by threats to the basic needs themselves. In Maslow's words, "These conditions are not ends in themselves, but they are almost so since they are so closely related to the basic needs, which are apparently the only end in themselves. These conditions are defended because without them the basic satisfactions are quite impossible, or at least, severely endangered." [1]

For some time Maslow has recognized a deficiency in his motivational theory. It has seemed inadequate to explain why, if the entire human species is growth-oriented, so many fail to develop their potential. Recently his thinking has crystallized, and he has added "challenge" (stimulation) as an additional precondition in the external environment. He now contends that, simultaneously and paradoxically, there is an innate human tendency toward inertia, as well as toward growth and activity. He explains this in part as being physiological—the need for rest, or recovery. But it is also a psychological response, a tendency to conserve energy. Scientific confirmation for this concept can be found in the extensive research of the late George Kingsley Zipf, Ph.D., as outlined in his book, *Human Behavior and the Principle of Least Effort.* [4]

Further Characteristics of the Basic Needs

The basic needs are generally discovered and desired in the order listed. However, there are many exceptions. Some individuals, for example, may prefer or seek self-esteem more than love from others. Or, the person who has been unemployed a long time may have lost or dulled the desire for higher needs after years of seeking only food. The psychopathic personality is one where, apparently, the love and affection needs have been so thoroughly frustrated that the desire to give and receive love and affection is lost. There are, of course, many historical examples of people who become martyrs to an idea, in complete disregard for their own basic needs.

People who have been fortunate enough to be born to circumstances enabling them to satisfy their basic needs develop such strong unified characters that they can then withstand the loss or frustration of these needs for considerable lengths of time. Gratification of these needs very early in life, especially the first two years, is very important; as Maslow says, "People who have been made secure and strong in the early years, tend to remain secure and strong thereafter in the face of whatever threatens." [1]

Maslow also cautions against viewing the hierarchy of needs too precisely. One must not assume that the need for security does not emerge until the need for food is entirely satisfied, or that the need for love does not emerge until the need for safety is fully satisfied. Most people in our society have partially satisfied most of their basic needs, but still have some unsatisfied basic needs remaining. It is the unsatisfied needs which have the greatest influence on behavior. Once a need has been gratified it has little effect on motivation. "A want that is satisfied is no longer a want." [1]

People may or may not be aware of their basic needs. "In the average person they are more often unconscious than conscious. . . . , although they may, with suitable techniques, and with sophisticated people, become conscious." [1] Behavior, as has been previously discussed, is the result of many forces. It may be a result, not only of several of the basic needs in combination, but also of personal habits, past experience, individual talents and capacities, and the external environment. "If in response to the stimulus word 'table,' I immediately perceive a memory image of a table, or think of a chair, this response has nothing to do with my basic needs." [1]

Perhaps only a person knowledgeable in previous theories of psychology can fully understand how radical these ideas are to the majority of behavioral scientists. Maslow described it as "the collapse around my ears of long-established, firmly believed-in and seemingly unassailable laws of psychology. . . . Truth, goodness and beauty are in the average person in our culture, only fairly well correlated with each other, and in the neurotic person even less so. It is only in the evolved and mature human being, in the self-actualizing, fully functioning person that they are so highly correlated that for all practical purposes they may be said to fuse into a unity. I would now add that this is also true for other people in their peak experiences.

"This finding, if it turns out to be correct, is in direct and flat contradiction to one of the basic axioms that guides all scientific thought, namely that the more objective and impersonal perception becomes, the more detached it becomes from value. Fact and value have almost always (by intellectuals) been considered to be antonyms and mutually exclusive." [3]

The Growth Needs

On the preceding pages we have catalogued the basic psychological needs as identified and listed by Dr. Maslow in his classic text, *Motivation and Personality*. As a result of further research, he enlarged and clarified the basic need theory in *Toward a Psychology of Being*.

What Maslow discovered was a whole new list of needs in a still higher category, which he described as growth needs (Being-values or B-values), as contrasted with the basic or deficiency needs. He said that this higher nature of man needed the lower nature as a foundation, and without which the higher nature "collapsed." "The major emphasis in humanistic psychology," he stated, "rests on the assumptions regarding 'higher needs.' They are seen as biologically based, part of the human essence . . ." [5] Thus, man is initially motivated by a series of basic needs; as these are satisfied, he moves toward the level of the higher needs and becomes motivated by them. As mentioned before, Maslow's term for this is meta-motivation.

There was a difference in these higher needs and the people who behaved on this higher plane, which Maslow found very difficult to describe. He found that such people, rather than struggling or coping with life, were spontaneous, expressive, natural, and free, almost as if they had got to the top of the hill and were now coasting down the other side. These values could not be fully separated from one another. They were all interrelated, and in defining one it was necessary to use the others. This is a list of the Being-values as Maslow found them:

"1. wholeness; (unity; integration; tendency to oneness; interconnectedness simplicity; organization; structure; dichotomy-transcendence; order);

2. perfection (necessity; just-right-ness; just-so-ness; inevitability; suitability; justice; completeness; "oughtness");

3. completion (ending; finality; justice; "it's finished"; fulfillment; finis and telos; destiny; fate);

4. justice (fairness; orderliness; lawfulness; "oughtness");

5. aliveness (process; non-deadness; spontaneity; self-regulation; full-functioning);

6. richness (differentiation; complexity; intricacy);

7. simplicity (honesty; nakedness; essentiality; abstract; essential; skeletal structure);

8. beauty (rightness; form; aliveness; simplicity; richness; wholeness; perfection; completion; uniqueness; honesty);

9. goodness (rightness; desirability; oughtness; justice; benevolence; honesty);

10. uniqueness (idiosyncrasy; individuality; noncomparability; novelty);

11. effortlessness (ease; lack of strain, striving or difficulty; grace; perfect, beautiful functioning);

12. playfulness (fun; joy; amusement; gaiety; humor; exuberance; effortlessness);

13. truth, honesty; reality (nakedness; simplicity; richness; oughtness; beauty; pure, clean and unadulterated; completeness; essentiality);

14. self-sufficiency (autonomy; independence; not needing-other-than-itself-in-order-to-be-itself; self-determining; environment-transcendence; separateness; living by its own laws)." [3]

Supporting Evidence

When *Motivation and Personality* was published in 1954 the book listed at least twelve major areas of support for the basic need theory. Since that time Dr. Maslow has continued to add even more evidence.

The first and foremost reason for advancing a new, comprehensive theory of motivation was the failure of earlier theories to solve human problems or explain all the known facts. ". . . clinical psychologists, psychiatrists, psycho-analysts, social workers, and all other clinicians use Behavioristic theory almost not at all. They proceed stubbornly in an *ad hoc* way to build an extensive, practical structure on inadequate theoretical foundations. They tend to be practical men rather than theorists." [1] Behaviorists, for example, hold that the need for love is an acquired or learned need, rather than innate. "Common experience supports such a contention almost not at all." [1] Dr. Maslow adds, "No single experiment known to the writer has ever been performed that shows this to be true for the needs for love, safety, belongingness, respect, understanding, etc." [1]

A number of clinical experiments—those of W. Goldfarb, for example—demonstrate that institutionalized children show psychopathological symptoms when they are not loved, in spite of the fact that all other physiological needs are well satisfied. "It should be an overwhelmingly impressive point that almost every school of psychiatry, psychoanalysis, clinical psychology, social work or child therapy has had to postulate some doctrine of instincts or instinct-like needs, no matter how much they disagreed on every other point." [1]

Ashley Montagu, the renowned anthropologist, has pointed out, "There is now good evidence which leads us to believe that not only does a baby want to be loved, but also that it wants to love, that all of its drives are oriented in the direction of receiving and giving love, and that if it doesn't receive love it is unable to give it—as a child or as an adult." [6]

Montagu also refers to several surveys early in the 20th Century that produced some shocking statistics. A typical one: "Dr. Henry Chapin reported on ten infant asylums located in the United States in which, with one exception, *every* infant under two years of age died." [6] Dr. Montagu attributes this disaster to the fact that these babies were not loved.

Maslow's basic need theory is also supported by hundreds of experiments with animals which have demonstrated their "wisdom of the body."

Examples of this are profusely described in Walter Kennon's book, *Wisdom of the Body*, (Norton, 1932), and also the free choice experiments of Kurt Richter which showed that animals who had lost their adrenal glands were able to alter their diet and remain alive. He also reported that a child with an adrenal tumor was able to keep himself alive by instinctively eating huge amounts of salt.

W. F. Dove found that when chickens were allowed to choose their own diets there was a wide variety of choices. Some chickens were better choosers than others and became larger and healthier. When the poor-choosing chickens were fed the same diet as the good choosers they, too, became larger, stronger, and healthier, although they did not usually overtake the good choosers.

D. M. Levy experimented with puppies and various needs, such as suckling. He found that when a need was fully gratified it either disappeared or maintained a low level for the rest of the life of the animal. But, when the need was frustrated, the animals developed psychopathological symptoms. This experimentation was repeated with other animals, including human babies, producing similar results. Levy also demonstrated the need of infants for love and tender care if they were to develop into mature adults. Levy studied the family backgrounds of healthy and neurotic people and found that healthy adults had not been deprived in the satisfaction of their basic needs when very young.

Anthropology, formerly dominated by Behavioristic theory, has in recent years uncovered considerable evidence to support Maslow's contention that the "ultimate desires of all human beings do not differ nearly as much as do their conscious everyday desires." [1] And this is so regardless of race or culture. "Within anthropology," he says, "the first rumbles of dissatisfaction with cultural relativism came from field workers who felt that it implied more profound and irreconcilable differences between people than actually existed." [1]

Dr. Maslow found a "gold mine" of evidence for his theory of basic needs in clinical practice—his own experience and that of hundreds of other therapists. His experience consistently showed that individuals who satisfy their basic needs are healthier, happier, and more effective, while those whose needs are frustrated develop psychopathological symptoms. Frustration of unimportant desires—desires which are apparently not basic needs—does not produce unhealthy symptoms, although Behaviorist theory maintains that the thwarting of any needs would. Therapists who seek to uncover the person's real self—Carl Rogers, Erich Fromm, and Karen Horney, for example—find that their methods increase love, courage, and creativity and reduce fear and hostility. This indicates that these traits must be inherent in the individual; otherwise, where do they come from? As Carl Rogers puts it: "The deeper I go into myself as an individual, the more I find my commonness with other individuals." [7] "If insight makes it [a trait] stronger," says Maslow, "we may thereafter consider it to be intrinsic." [1] "Also, as Horney has reasoned, if the release of anxiety causes the patient to become more affectionate and less hostile, does this not indicate that affection is basic to human nature, while hostility is not?" [1]

All of this may be summed up in the statement that the frustration of basic needs creates psychopathological symptoms, and their satisfaction leads to healthy personalities, both psychologically and biologically. The study of self-actualizing people proves again and again that such people, regardless of their cultures, value the same things. The peak experiences (described in Chapter five) provide evidence that even average individuals have moments when they are "hitting on all cylinders." The fact that they value the higher needs during these peak experiences suggests the genetic origin of basic needs.

In his early training as a Behaviorist, Maslow was taught that people had cognitive abilities, but no mention was made of cognitive *needs*. It was research by one of his professors, E. L. Thorndyke, which started Maslow thinking that perhaps people had a need to know, as well as the ability to know. Thorndyke and some of his colleagues had studied a group of children of extremely high I.Q.s—over 180. The researchers found that every child in this group had shown an almost insatiable curiosity, which needed no encouragement, but manifested itself as a powerful hunger or drive or need.

H. Harlow and his students performed a series of experiments with monkeys which showed that they would put a great deal of effort into the solution of puzzles even when no reward was forthcoming. The only possible explanation seemed to be that the monkeys had an innate curiosity, and it gave them satisfaction to solve puzzles.

The tendency of the human species to seek growth and self-actualization has been observed and reported "by thinkers as diverse as Aristotle

ABRAHAM MASLOW'S HIERARCHY OF NEEDS

SELF ACTUALIZATION

GROWTH NEEDS *
(*Being values*)
(*Metaneeds*)

TRUTH
GOODNESS
BEAUTY
ALIVENESS
INDIVIDUALITY
PERFECTION
NECESSITY
COMPLETION
JUSTICE
ORDER
SIMPLICITY
RICHNESS
PLAYFULNESS
EFFORTLESSNESS
SELF SUFFICIENCY
MEANINGFULNESS

SELF ESTEEM
ESTEEM BY OTHERS

LOVE & BELONGINGNESS

BASIC NEEDS
(*Deficiency needs*)
SAFETY AND SECURITY

PHYSIOLOGICAL
AIR, WATER, FOOD, SHELTER, SLEEP, SEX

THE EXTERNAL ENVIRONMENT
PRECONDITIONS FOR NEED SATISFACTION
FREEDOM, JUSTICE, ORDERLINESS
CHALLENGE (STIMULATION)

* Growth needs are all of equal importance (not hierarchical)

and Bergson, and by many other philosophers. Among psychiatrists, psycho-analysts and psychologists it has been found necessary by Goldstein, Rank, Jung, Horney, Fromm, May, and Rogers." [1]

Maslow was aware that Eastern philosophy, in particular, confirmed his point of view and that Aristotle had written a great deal about the "good life." "We may agree with Aristotle when he assumed that the good life consisted in living in accordance with the true nature of man," Maslow said, "but we must add that he simply did not know enough about the true nature of man. . . . If one observes human beings only on the surface, which was all Aristotle could do, one must ultimately wind up with what amounts to a static conception of human nature." [1] For example, Maslow pointed out that Aristotle completely accepted the fact of slavery and, hence, made the fatal error of assuming that because a man was a slave his essential nature was slave-like; and, therefore, it was good for him to be a slave.

CHAPTER 5

Human Potential

Very early in the 20th Century, William James, one of America's most distinguished psychologist-philosophers, concluded that the average individual was using only a small part of his full potential. James considered this one of his most important discoveries. "Compared to what we ought to be, we are only half awake. Our fires are dampened, our drafts are checked, we are making use of only a small part of our mental and physical resources." For some reason psychiatrists and behavioral scientists lost sight of this important conclusion—probably because of the orientation of the disciplines toward the study of mental illness, "the average," and animals. Whatever the reasons, very little has been done in the last fifty or sixty years to study human potential and how to develop it. As recently as 1967, Dr. Herbert Otto, a social psychologist who has pioneered in this area stated, ". . . the topic of human potentialities has, for the last 50 years, been almost totally ignored as a focus of research activity by workers in the social and behavioral sciences." [1]

Belief that the human species has a great deal of unrealized potential is an important aspect of Dr. Maslow's comprehensive theory of human motivation. He believes that all or, at least, nearly all babies are born with the potential and the need to grow psychologically.

By studying the best of humanity, the less-than-one per cent at the top, we get an idea what man's potential really is. Most, if not all, of the human species, Maslow believes, have a need for and a tendency toward self-actualization. In spite of the fact that apparently all have this potential, only a tiny percentage is now achieving it. This is, in part, because people are blind to their potential; they neither know what is possible nor understand the rewards of self-actualization.

One example Maslow cites is that of the Olympic gold medal winner. The champion demonstrates what the potential in his specialty is, and holds this up as a standard for all other athletes. When Maslow was a youngster trying to compete on the track team, it was considered a human impossibility to run a mile in less than four minutes. Eventually, what was humanly "impossible" became possible because people proved that it *was* possible. And with each new record the human potential in these events increases.

Maslow's concept of man does not rule out the probability of genetic differences at birth; however, it recognizes that species-wide potentials exist as well. These great potentials exist in each human being, but are difficult to measure. "We cannot measure how tall a person might become, only how tall he is. Never how intelligent he could be under best conditions, only how intelligent he is under actually existing conditions." [2] Thus, all we can do is look to these outstanding people, these "Olympic medal winners," who broaden our horizons.

Maslow believes that most individuals have a capacity for creativeness, spontaneity, caring for others, curiosity, continual growth, the ability to love and be loved, and all of the other characteristics found in self-actualized people. A person who is behaving badly is reacting to the deprivation of his basic needs. If his behavior improves he begins to develop his true potential and move toward greater health and normality as a human. Freud, says Maslow, taught us that past experience exists in the present in each individual. "Now we must learn from the growth theory and self-actualization theory that the future also *now* exists in the person in the form of ideals, hopes, duties, tasks, plans, goals, unrealized potentials, mission, fate, destiny, etc." [3]

Maslow encourages his graduate students to set high levels of aspiration. He will ask them what great book or great task they are planning to accomplish. This type of questioning tends to embarrass students, and they seek to evade it. But Maslow asks, "If you plan to be a psychologist, do you plan to be active or inactive; good or bad? If you do not aspire to write the great new classic, who will? If you deliberately plan to be less than you are capable of being, then I warn you that you'll be unhappy for the rest of your life. You will be evading your own capacities, your own possibilities." [4]

It takes a certain type of arrogance and dreams of the grandiose for an individual to say he will surpass Plato, and the person who sets such a high goal is bound to have moments of weakness because he knows his own imperfections. But he should realize that Plato himself must have had similar moments of doubt, uncertainty, and weakness, but pushed on regardless. Maslow warns that we must not become unrealistic about human potential. There is a trend toward growth in human nature, but we must also recognize a counter trend, a tendency to regress, to fear growth, to fail to self-actualize.

One of Dr. Maslow's discoveries in his study of self-actualizing individuals was the fact that they reported what he called "peak experiences"—moments when they felt at their very best, moments of great awe, intense happiness, rapture, bliss, or ecstasy. Gradually it became apparent that peak experiences were not occurring exclusively to psychologically healthy people; apparently most individuals can and frequently do have peak experiences. Maslow found that the best question to ask people was to describe "the single most joyous, happiest, most blissful moment of your whole life." [5]

Thus, a peak experience is a moment in the individual's life when he is functioning fully, feels strong, sure of himself, and in complete control. A comparison might be made with an engine that suddenly hits on all cylinders and performs perfectly, producing a real surge of power; whereas, it had been missing, sputtering, and running poorly. Inventors, great athletes, leaders, and executives exhibit this type of behavior when functioning at their peak. The person in peak experience is more decisive, stronger, single-minded, able to withstand opposition, sure of himself. To the observer, this person looks more reliable, dependable, and trustworthy.

It is sometimes possible to recognize this moment in therapy. Carl

Rogers described the peak experience as "fully-functioning." During this period of integration and unity the individual is more spontaneous, more and more expressive, and there is a feeling of being free of the past and the future. During these moments of great happiness, doubts, fears, inhibitions, temptations, and weaknesses are absent—also feelings of self-consciousness.

Peak experiences may be brought about by many causes: listening to great music, a great athletic achievement, a good sexual experience, even dancing. "It looks as if any experience of real excellence, of real perfection, of any moving toward the perfect justice or toward perfect values, tends to produce a peak experience." [5]

Some examples from Dr. Maslow's files are as follows: "A young mother was scurrying around her kitchen and getting breakfast for her husband and young children. The sun was streaming in, the children, clean and nicely dressed, were chattering as they ate. The husband was casually playing with the children; but, as she looked at them she was suddenly so overwhelmed with their beauty and her great love for them, and her feeling of good fortune, that she went into a peak-experience.

"A young man working his way through medical school by drumming in a jazz band reported years later, that in all his drumming he had three peaks when he suddenly felt like a great drummer and his performance was perfect.

"A hostess after a dinner party where everything had gone perfectly and it had been a fine evening, said good-bye to her last guest, sat down in a chair, looked around at the mess, and went into a peak of great happiness and exhilaration." [6]

Not only does the person having peak experience feel better, stronger, and more unified, but the world looks better, more unified, and honest. For an average person a peak experience can be a fleeting glimpse of what self-actualization is. From a variety of descriptions from perhaps one hundred different individuals, Maslow made a list of some of the words which seem to be common to peak experiences, regardless of their source. The list, as can be seen, is identical to the Being-values of a self-actualizing person. They are "truth, beauty, wholeness, dichotomy-transcendance, aliveness-process, uniqueness, perfection, necessity, completion, justice, order, simplicity, richness, effortlessness, playfulness, and self-sufficiency." [3]

Peak experiences may have beneficial therapeutic effects—that is, the removal of neurotic symptoms. Maslow has received several reports from psychologists and others about peak experiences which were so profound as to permanently remove certain symptoms. Under the right conditions these experiences can change people in a permanent way. Working with alcoholics, Dr. A. Hoffer tried to induce peak experiences for therapeutic purposes. Music, visual stimuli, suggestions, mescaline, and L.S.D. were used to give the alcoholics peak experiences. It was found that the majority of alcoholics who were able to conquer their problem reported peak experiences, while almost none of those who did not have peak experiences were able to reform.

Most people, Dr. Maslow found, did not readily talk about their moments of great joy and ecstacy. They were not the types of experiences people spoke of in public. Many were embarrassed or ashamed because these experiences were not "scientific." Many people, during and after these moments of joy, felt very fortunate and grateful, and, as a result, felt a love for others and the world, and even had a desire to do something good in the world as repayment. Maslow found peak experiences to have most of the characteristics traditionally ascribed to religious experiences from nearly every creed and faith. "Is it not meaningful also that the mystic experience has been described in almost identical words by people in every religion, every era, and in every culture?" [3]

William James called these "mystic experiences" [7] and described them in detail. Maslow reports that the descriptions of these experiences by religious people and by people who do not consider themselves religious seem to be almost identical, and thus, believes it is possible to dissociate this experience from any supernatural reference, because it is a natural experience as well. Freud, who was an atheist, also described it and called it "the oceanic feeling."

Maslow concludes that during the peak experience people have a better perception of reality itself. During these moments people have the same insights that many philosophers and theologians have had regarding the unifying aspects of reality.

CHAPTER 6

Psychological Growth

Closely related to Abraham Maslow's ideas on potential is his concept of growth. His research led him to conclude that growth toward self-actualization is both natural and necessary. By growth he means constant development of talents, capacities, creativity, wisdom, and character. Growth is the progressive satisfaction of higher and higher levels of psychological needs. In Maslow's words, "Man demonstrates in his own nature a pressure toward fuller and fuller being, more and more perfect actualization of his humanness in exactly the same naturalistic scientific sense that an acorn may be said to be 'pressing toward' being an oak tree." [1]

Evidence for this conclusion was the discovery that psychological growth led to psychological health, while people who failed to grow suffered from symptoms of mental and physical pathology.

Orthodox Behaviorist theory has assumed that the human species seeks an equilibrium, seeks to reduce tension, and that most behavior can be defined in tension-reducing terms. Freud also believed in tension-reduction and the pleasure-pain principle, saying that the human species constantly sought pleasure and avoided pain. Maslow, however, reports that more and more psychologists and behavioral scientists are being forced to assume a human tendency toward growth and self-actualization, because the tension-reduction theories do not adequately explain human behavior. Or, as Maslow said, "If the motivational life consists essentially of a defensive removal of irritating tensions, and if the only end product of tension-reduction is a state of passive waiting for more unwelcome irritations to arise and in their turn, to be dispelled, then how does change or development or movement or direction come about? Why do people improve? Get wiser? What does zest in living mean?" [1]

Historically, such great, yet diverse thinkers as Plato, Aristotle, Bergson, and other leading philosophers had reached this conclusion, as well as many psychiatrists and psychologists. Maslow said, "All the evidence that we have (mostly clinical evidence, but already some other kinds of research evidence) indicates that it is reasonable to assume in practically every human being, certainly in almost every newborn baby, that there is an active will toward health, an impulse toward growth, or toward the actualization of human potentialities." [2]

Man has the capacity to grow, and yet, according to Dr. Maslow's research, only a small percentage of people even in our relatively free American society come anywhere near realization of their full potentials. Maslow suggests a number of reasons why so many fail to grow.

1. As mentioned, man's instincts toward growth are weak rather than strong, and thus growth tendencies can be easily stifled by bad habits, a poor cultural environment, or inadequate—even erroneous—education.

2. There has been a strong tendency in western culture to fear instincts, to believe they are all animalistic and bad. Freud and many Christian theorists have stressed the negative aspects of human instincts, and, as a result, we have a culture emphasizing controls and negative motivation rather than positive motivation.

3. There is the strong negative influence of the lower needs for safety and security. The growth process requires constant willingness to take chances, to make mistakes, to break habits. "One can choose," says Maslow, "to go back toward safety or forward toward growth. Growth must be chosen again and again; fear must be overcome again and again." [3] "Anything that increases fear or anxiety tips the dynamic balance between regression and growth back toward regression and away from growth." [4]

Children in a secure, warm, friendly atmosphere are more apt to grow and learn the growth process. Children in insecure surroundings seek safety. Even a healthy child, when placed in strange surroundings, will become more cautious, less apt to explore, etc.

4. Maslow advanced what he called the "Jonah" complex: the tendency in adults to doubt and even fear their own abilities, their own potential to be greater. "We fear our highest possibilities (as well as our lowest ones). We are generally afraid to become that which we can glimpse in our most perfect moments, under the most perfect conditions, under conditions of greatest courage. We enjoy and even thrill to the godlike possibilities we see in ourselves in such peak moments. And yet we simultaneously shiver with weakness, awe, and fear for these very same possibilities." [2]

The individual who is growing is constantly challenging himself. This takes courage. When man steps into a new and better situation he can't help but have an uneasy feeling of inadequacy, and some people never learn how to overcome this fear. The pleasures of growth and development require effort, self-discipline, and a certain amount of pain. The person who is Freudian in outlook, that is, one who seeks pleasure and avoids pain, is not nearly so apt to grow. What Freud observed was certainly true for many people, especially the unhealthy specimens he studied.

5. The cultural environment can and often does stifle human development toward self-actualization. One example is the common cultural concept of what is manly and what is not. Such human aspects as sympathy, kindness, gentleness, and tenderness are frequently discouraged because of this cultural tendency to consider such characteristics unmanly.

6. We have already reported the discovery that self-actualizing people are more flexible than the average, more open to new ideas and new experiences. Conversely, it follows that habits are obstacles to growth. Most people exhibit strong tendencies to continue to do as they have in the past. This is not always bad; there are many types of habits which release the mind for other activities. At the same time other habits formed, sometimes early in life and never re-examined, limit the individual's development. "However useful habits may be for constant aspects of the world, they are positively a hindrance and impediment when the organism has to deal with the changing, fluctuating aspects of the world with problems which are unique, novel, never before met with. . . . Preference for the famil-

iar becomes a life and death necessity in abnormal cases. The healthy taste for the novel and unknown is missing or at a minimum in the average neurotic." [5]

In our consideration of the failure to grow we have hinted at the methods for growth. For the healthy child in the healthy environment, growth seems to be encouraged by giving the child freedom to explore and freedom to learn through trial and error. The same applies to the adult. Overprotection and coddling can easily become growth-inhibiting; people need to learn to make their own choices; when the choices are constantly made by others growth will certainly be inhibited. Maslow believes that growth requires a certain amount of pain and sorrow and that we must learn not always to protect children or adults from such painful but necessary experiences.

Recently, Maslow has added still another possible explanation for man's frequent failure to develop his potential. Basing his conclusions on the work of Dr. Zipf and his own observations, Dr. Maslow now recognizes a tendency toward a certain inertia in the individual—what Dr. Zipf termed "the principle of least effort."

Self-knowledge and self-understanding, in his opinion, are the most important roads toward self-actualization—a process which can be aided or thwarted by parents, teachers, and the cultural environment. Professional therapists who understand the growth process can be tremendously helpful. When a person understands himself he will understand his basic needs and his true motivation and learn to behave in a manner which will satisfy those needs. Self-understanding will also enable one to understand and relate to other people more effectively. If the entire human species has the same basic needs, then it follows that self-understanding leads to understanding of the entire human species.

The development of courage, integrity, and self-respect are important to continual growth. Maslow learned from his experience with graduate students at Brandeis that freedom (permissiveness) could be growth-producing for some, but for others seemed to produce negative results. It was what he called the "continental-divide principle"—it either made them or broke them. For the already-healthy individual, stress and challenge were growth-producing; but for the insecure, weak individual this was not the answer. Apparently people can be benefited by challenge only if the challenge does not exceed their personal limits. "This means," says

Maslow "more research than we now have on the good effects of discipline and the bad effects of indulgence, the good effects of frustration, the good effects of hardship, the good effects of challenge, etc." [4]

Self-actualizers cannot avoid discipline and a certain amount of control, but it is far better when this is self-imposed rather than external. However, as the individual develops, the need for control lessens, and actions become more natural and spontaneous. An example is the artist who struggles and works to become skillful, until all the techniques are mastered, and his art becomes free and spontaneous. Most religions and moral philosophies, Maslow believes, put too much stress on control and will power and too little stress on self-understanding and spontaneity. Aristotle, for example, proposed a hierarchy of human capacities with reason at the peak. Maslow contends that, for the healthy person, subjective feeling must be given greater recognition and respect.

It seems evident that people who have been loved, particularly in childhood, are more apt to grow in a healthy way than those who have been deprived of love. Nearly all schools of thought now tend to agree on this point.

Satisfaction of the lower needs for food, clothing, and shelter does not in itself guarantee growth. "It is a great mystery to me why affluence releases some people for growth while permitting other people to stay fixated at a strictly 'materialistic' level. . . . it may turn out to be useful to add to the definition of the self-actualizing person, not only that he be 1. sufficiently free of illness, 2. that he be sufficiently gratified in his basic needs, and 3. that he be positively using his capacities, but also 4. that he be motivated by some values which he strives for or gropes for and to which he is loyal." [6]

Freud was generally contemptuous of values. To him right behavior was uninhibited behavior—uninhibited expression of the animal drive for survival. To the Behaviorists and the vast majority of behavioral scientists, values are considered completely outside the realm of the scientific study of human nature. To the majority of scientists, science and moral relativism are synonymous.

Under healthy conditions growth is rewarding and the healthy individual grows for this reason. Healthy growth encourages growth, and the more one grows, the more one wants to grow. " . . . the process of moment-to-moment growth is itself intrinsically rewarding and delightful in

an absolute sense." [1] Maslow deplores the modern tendency to model ourselves after the "well-adjusted man. . . . Every age but ours has had its
model, its ideal. All of these have been given up by our culture; the saint,
the hero, the gentleman, the knight, the mystic. About all we have left is
the well-adjusted man without problems, a very pale and doubtful substitute. Perhaps we shall soon be able to use as our guide and model the fully
growing and self-filling human being, the one in whom all his potentialities are coming to full development, the one whose inner nature expresses
itself freely, rather than being warped, suppressed, or denied." [1]

CHAPTER 7

Third Force
Education

Considering Dr. Maslow's interest in all aspects of human behavior and his own experience as a father, it is only natural that he would have much to say about child development. Because of important differences between his explanation of human nature and the two other major theories, Maslow's work calls for a new examination of child-raising theory.

All three theories recognize the importance of the early years in character formation. Also, an increasing number of psychologists and psychiatrists, regardless of their theoretical background, recognize the importance of love and respect in the parent-child situation. Maslow says that, if the parents treat the child with love and respect, they can make a lot of mistakes and still be successful. The type of child-rearing he recommends is perhaps best described as freedom-with-limits. He recognizes the danger of complete permissiveness or parental indulgence and, at the same time, recognizes the damaging effect of the dictatorial, authoritarian parent who squelches, controls, or overprotects the child until he is unable to develop a personality of his own. Successful parents need to know when to say yes and when to say no. As Maslow points out, there is increasing evidence that even young children, when healthy, have a certain "internal wisdom," which enables them to make good dietary choices, to know when they are ready to be weaned, to know how much sleep they need, to know when they are ready for toilet training, and so forth. What we are learning, he says, is to "give the baby a choice; we let him decide. We offer him both the liquid and the solid food. If the solid appeals to him he will spontaneously wean himself from the breast. In the same way we have learned to let the child tell us when he needs love, or protection, or respect, or control, but setting up a permissive, accepting, satisfying atmosphere." [1]

Professor Maslow explains that this does not mean permissiveness under all conditions and with all children. It works with healthy children; it may not work with those who have already developed character problems. Freudian theory saw every child as resisting change and growth and, thus, requiring continual pushing or kicking out of his comfortable state into a new, frightening situation. Maslow flatly contradicts this concept. Although it is true for some insecure, frightened children, it is not true for healthy children. "Observation of children shows more and more clearly that healthy children *enjoy* growing and moving forward, gaining new skills, capacities, and powers." [2]

This idea of more freedom in child raising must be balanced by the need to teach the child discipline and respect for others—a value system.

In an article published in *Harper's Magazine*, 1960, Maslow compares child raising and delinquency in the United States and Mexico. He points out that there is less juvenile delinquency, vandalism, and destruction in Mexico, and juvenile-gang attacks upon adults are virtually unknown. The usual explanations of American sociologists (Behaviorists) do not seem to apply, because Mexican children are deprived even to the point of hunger. Maslow believes that in Mexican culture there is more agreement on values, on what is right and wrong; because the adults are less confused, children grow up less confused. The father is the leader in the home, and he does not hesitate to set rules of deportment, which the wife supports, and the child must follow. "By comparison, the American parent is confused, uncertain, guilty, and conflicted. His traditions have gone and no new ones are yet available to him." [3]

In Mexican culture, it is customary for the male adult to provide some definition of right and wrong behavior. In recent years American fathers have tended, in many cases, to abdicate their role of structuring the world for the child. This tends to result in an insecure, anxious, and frequently hostile child. The child develops contempt and resentment against his parents, particularly the father who is frustrating his need for order and values. Under the circumstances children turn to other sources—this may be other children, usually older ones. The child needs freedom to grow, to learn, to discover himself, to develop skills; but he also needs the security of rules and limits, an opportunity to learn, to control, to denounce, to tolerate frustration, and to become self-disciplined. "Only to the self-disciplined and responsible person can we say 'do as you will and it will probably be all right.'" [2]

The child needs to learn the proper way to gratify his basic needs; he must understand that other human beings must be allowed to satisfy their needs. The proper educational process should be concerned with the growth and development of the child, not just restraining and subduing him for the convenience of adults. Maslow says we must learn more about how to teach children strength, self-respect, righteous indignation, resistance to domination and exploitation, to propaganda and untruth.

Education, both formal and informal, plays an important role in the development of character. We need to know more about how this can best be done—whether in the classroom: through books, lectures, catechisms, sermons; or through love, respect, and proper treatment. The first two years have a great deal of significance. The child who feels strong and secure in these early years tends to retain that strength and security in the face of future threats.

The average deprived child "keeps on pressing for admiration, for safety, autonomy, for love, etc., in whatever childish way he can invent. The ordinary action of the sophisticated adult is to say 'oh, he's just showing off,' or 'he's only trying to get attention,' and thereupon to banish him from the adult company. That is to say, this diagnosis is customarily interpreted as an injunction *not* to give the child what he is seeking, *not* to notice, *not* to admire, *not* to applaud.

"If, however, we should come to consider such pleas for acceptance, love, or admiration as legitimate demands of the same order as complaints of hunger, thirst, cold, or pain, we should automatically become gratifiers rather than frustrators. The single consequence of such a regime would be that both children and parents would have more fun." [1] This is quite different from what Maslow describes as "the present wave of child centering," which means giving in to the child whenever and whatever he wants, being afraid to frustrate him by saying no when no is the proper answer. "In the U.S. . . . the father is not only afraid of his wife, but of his children as well (and is therefore often afraid to punish, to refuse, to frustrate." [3]

Parents must avoid overprotection and overindulgence to the extent that the child's every need is provided for him without any effort on his part. Such a child is unable to develop strength and self-reliance. It may produce a person who tends to use other people, rather than respect them. Such indulgence shows a lack of respect for the child and his potential to develop. Under these circumstances the child may develop an attitude of worthlessness.

The over-protected, insecure child tends to cling to the mother, who represents safety and protection; but, because of this, fails to explore, to venture, to learn, to develop. "There are plenty of data to indicate that a mother who truly and deeply loves her child can behave in practically any way toward that child, beating or slapping it, or whatever, and yet the child will turn out well." [4] A good parent has some of the characteristics of a good leader, enough personal strength to "take pleasure in the growth and self-actualization of other people . . . if one had to define a father, very briefly it would be about the same way in which I've defined the perfect boss." [4] The father should be honest and open with his wife and family; yet, there are times when he needs to keep his troubles, doubts, fears, and anxieties to himself, rather than confessing all his weaknesses to the family.

The self-actualized person does not always find it easy to be a good parent; his very competence can be discouraging to his children. Most child psychology, says Dr. Maslow, puts too much stress on the child's need to love. It is inadequate, he says, to stress that children will behave well in order to receive the love of their parents. It is equally true that children will behave well because they love their parents. Providing it is not indulgence, love is hard to oversupply. "For a child who has not been loved enough," he says, "obviously the treatment of first choice is to love him to death, to just slop it all over him. Clinical and general human experience is that it works." [5]

Maslow rejects the tendency of Freudian psychology to picture the young child as selfish, destructive, aggressive, and uncooperative. Normal children, he says, can be hostile, destructive, and selfish, but they can also be generous, cooperative, and unselfish. Whether they will show more of the first and less of the second depends upon the climate in which they are raised. If they are insecure, threatened, frustrated in satisfaction of their basic needs, the negative aspects will predominate. If they are loved and respected, they will show far less destructive and aggressive behavior. Under some conditions, however, refusal to conform may be healthy rather than unhealthy. "Crime and delinquency and bad behavior in children may represent psychiatrically and biologically *legitimate* revolt against exploitation, injustice, and unfairness." [1]

The healthy child has a great deal of curiosity; in fact, if it is lacking, it is an indication of pathology. "There seems to be a general agreement (among all trained observers as well as among all parents) that the child shows inquisitive behavior at a very early age and that this behavior can be best explained by some sort of innate drive . . ." [6]

Third Force psychological theory calls for a new kind of education. This education will put more emphasis on development of the person's potential, particularly the potential to be human, to understand self and others and relate to them, to achieve the basic human needs, to grow toward self-actualization. This education will help "the person to become the best that he is able to become." [7]

Our present institutions and methods fall far short of the image Dr. Maslow projects. The educational process should be concerned with developing self discipline, spontaneity, and creativity at the same time. Students need to learn that high-sounding words like patriotism, democracy, and social progress mean people working hour by hour, day by day, at jobs which are a means to an end. There is a need, he says, "to teach the individual to examine reality directly and freshly." [1] Even graduate students do not have sufficient opportunity for first-hand observation; their instruction has become more and more the study of "what other people have done rather than the doing itself." [1] "There is no substitute for experience, none at all." [8]

All too often the process reduces rather than increases intuition and creativity, although some students have gained these characteristics through education. "There are the Ph.D.'s who are 'licensed fools.' " [8] The educational process should concern itself less with means and more with results; the development of understanding, judgment, good taste, the knowledge of how to live. The universities place more emphasis on courses on how to teach than they do on actual teaching experience; there is too much emphasis on theory, too little on practice. "Is a classroom really the only place or the best place to get educated? Is all knowledge conveyable in words? Can it all be put into books? Into courses and lectures? Can it always be measured by written tests? Must *any* mother defer to *any* child psychologist? Are ministers in charge of all religious experiences?" [8]

Instruction in the classroom should be related to life. The student should learn to grow, learn the difference between good and bad and what is desirable and undesirable and what to choose and not to choose. To acquire wisdom, maturity, taste, and character requires experience, trial and error, success, failure, disappointment, pain, marriage, having children. These are all important parts of the learning experience.

Theory, separated from experience and practice, can be very dangerous. On the other hand, the practical person who does not understand theory is also handicapped. Even these two aspects of knowledge are not enough without the third aspect: self-knowledge, self-understanding, the ability to feel subjectively. All of these aspects of knowledge are necessary for healthy growth. "Socrates taught that ultimately evil behavior can come only from ignorance. Here I am suggesting that good behavior needs as a precondition, good knowledge, and is perhaps a necessary consequence of good knowledge." [8]

Personally, Maslow found psychoanalysis very profitable. Prior to his marriage he had suffered depressed feelings. Analysis helped him to overcome this—to gain insight and self-understanding. He was helped to be less boyish and to become more mature. However, he learned that psychoanalysis itself does not perform all the miracles; eventually self-analysis takes over.

Psychology is constantly struggling with the problem of resistance to truth. The human species frequently seeks desperately to avoid truth which appears damaging to the ego. Courage and integrity are important characteristics in the person desiring psychological growth. "Experientially empty" is the phrase Maslow uses to describe people who are not able to perceive their own inner signals. An "experientially rich" person is a person who has great self-awareness. It is this characteristic of experiential richness which needs to be taught and developed. For, as Maslow says, ". . . what we are blind and deaf to within ourselves, we are also blind and deaf to in the outer world, whether it be playfulness, poetic feeling, aesthetic sensitivity, primary creativity, or the like." [9] When the total educational process is functioning properly, the student discovers more and more bits of truth about himself, other people, and the physical world and, in the process, sees increasing unity and becomes increasingly unified.

CHAPTER 8

Mental Illness

Dr. Maslow casts mental illness in a significantly different role than do many orthodox psychologists and psychiatrists. If mental health can be defined and is characteristic of the entire human species, then mental illness, whether we call it neurosis or psychosis or whatever, can be seen as a failure to achieve mental health. Thus mental illness is a deficiency disease, an inability of the individual to recognize and satisfy his species-wide needs.

Maslow's data, accumulated through twelve years of clinical practice and more than twenty years of research, indicated that most neuroses involved unsatisfied needs for security and relationships with others, such as respect, acceptance, and a feeling of belonging. The fact that the gratification of basic needs is primary to the successful cure or improvement of neuroses gives strong support to his Third Force psychology. Said in another way, the psychologically sick person is one who has never learned to achieve good human relations. Although the instinctoid needs are weak in the sense that they are easily ignored; in another sense they are very strong because failure to satisfy them results in psychological problems.

Most previous theories, particularly those of Freud and the Behaviorists, rested heavily on the concept of frustration; and frustration has usually been defined as simply not getting what one desires, interference with a wish and its gratification. "Such a definition," Maslow says, "fails to make the distinction between a deprivation that is unimportant to the organism (easily substituted for, with few serious after-effects) and, on the other hand, a deprivation that is at the same time a threat to the personality, that is, to the life goals of the individual, to his defensive system, to his self-esteem, to his self-actualization, i.e., to his basic needs. It is our contention that only a *threatening* deprivation has the multitude of effects (usually undesirable) that are commonly attributed to frustration in general." [1]

Alternate theories of neurosis fail to explain why some frustrations are damaging, others are not, and why some conflicts produce pathology, others do not. Even the word "neurosis" no longer is suitable; it implies an illness of the nerves and is based on a medical rather than a psychological model. If maturity is defined as fully-human, then mental illness may better be described as human diminution rather than neurosis—mental problems are the failures of personal growth. Thus, Dr. Maslow suggests, "it is better to consider neuroses as rather related to spiritual disorders, to loss of meaning, to doubts about the goals of life, to grief and anger over a lost love, to seeing life in a different way, to loss of courage or of hope, to despair over the future, to dislike for oneself, to recognition that one's life is being wasted, or that there is no possibility of joy or love, etc., etc. . . . These are all fallings away from full-humanness, from the full blooming of human nature." [2]

Most previous theories of mental disorder, following the "scientific" model lifted from the physical sciences, have attempted to ignore people's subjective feelings—their emotions, worries, and frustrations. And yet, it is in this very area that the neurotic pays the highest price for ignoring his own needs—needs which the "scientist" also ignores and denies. "Not only does the neurotic pay a huge subjective price for his vain attempt, (to neglect his own human nature) but ironically enough he also becomes progressively a poorer and poorer thinker." [1]

Such people are physically mature but psychologically retarded, never having overcome their childhood attitudes. A neurotic adult may still behave as if he were afraid of a spanking. People who fail to develop their talents, who live dull, uninteresting lives, who never develop workable methods of relating to other people, subconsciously know that they have wronged themselves for it. From this, "neurosis" develops.

There is an important difference between this viewpoint of psychopathology and the medical model that mental illness may be some type of invasion from without by a virus or whatever, which has no relationship to the behavior of the person being invaded. This medical model has the implication that there is not much the patient can do about this. He has not caused it; he cannot correct it. He must wait passively for doctors to provide the right medicine, as if he had a case of measles.

One of the important characteristics of the mentally healthy, self-actualizing individual is his realistic perception of the world. Conversely the disturbed person is not only emotionally sick, he is cognitively wrong as well. This description of mental disturbance is confirmed by the work of an English psychoanalyst, Money-Kyrle, who states that it seems best to recognize the neurotic person as not only relatively but absolutely inefficient, because his perception of reality is distorted.[1]

In Maslow's words, "Neurosis, psychosis, stunting of growth—all are, from this point of view, cognitive diseases as well, contaminating perception, learning, remembering, attending, and thinking."[3]

The individual who allows his desires to distort his perception diminishes his psychological health. In the truly mature individual reality is seen as it is, rather than as the individual wishes it were. Neurosis may also be recognized as the inability to choose wisely: that is, to choose in conformance with one's true psychological needs. People may be divided into good and bad choosers, just as chickens may be. Some people who are poor perceivers can believe in falsehoods year after year even though truth continually stares them in the face.

Psychosomatic research shows again and again that fear, anxiety, worry, and insecurity tend to develop undesirable physical and psychological results. These attitudes of anxiety, tension, and apprehensiveness are the result of safety-need frustration. Clinical observations show a significant difference between people who feel safe and secure and those who are unable to overcome fears. These neurotic adults, Maslow says, continue to behave like unsafe children.

From this point of view, one of Freud's greatest discoveries was that fear and guilt are root causes of much mental illness. Viewed in the light of new knowledge however, Freud's observations take on an entirely new meaning. Maslow finds that people do indeed repress and inhibit; they are afraid of themselves. Such fear is a failure of self-understanding. But there are two kinds of guilt: real guilt which is necessary and justified because of the individual's failure to be true to his own psychological needs, and neurotic guilt which was the only kind Freud recognized and which concerned the tendency of the individual to fear opinions and disapproval of other people.

Real guilt has a useful function: it directs the person toward personal growth; it functions as his conscience. The pain produced by real guilt tells the individual he is doing something that is bad for him. The deeply insecure person behaves just as Freud described: as an animal in the jungle. To him, the world is a dangerous place populated either by those he can dominate or by those who can dominate him, and the value system of such a person is derived from this view of the world. For many neurotic people the world is a bad place because they see it as dangerous, threatening, selfish, humiliating, and cold. Insecure people tend to behave in a way which makes their insecurity worse. That is, they behave in a way which makes people dislike and reject them, which makes them more insecure, which makes their behavior still more insecure—developing a vicious circle.

There are many ways in which this insecurity may express itself. Some insecure people are shy and withdrawn; others are hostile, aggressive, and nasty. One person may become a political extremist, for example, because he is insecure and perceives his personal difficulties as a world crisis. However, there is an entirely different type of extremist: one who is personally secure, happy, and contented, but deeply concerned about others. "The generally insecure person needs power, but this shows itself in many ways and in many different forms, such as overambition, overaggression, possessiveness, hunger for money, overcompetitiveness, tendency to prejudice and hatred, etc., or as their apparent opposites, e.g., bootlicking, submissiveness, masochistic trends, etc." [1]

People need to develop and use the talents they have in order to grow and self-actualize—this is mental health. As previously mentioned, Maslow found many clinical cases where the opposite existed; he found "intelligent people leading 'stupid lives'" which led to boredom, loss of zest, self-disapproval, and even physical deterioration. Such problems were particularly characteristic of women who were intelligent, prosperous, and unoccupied; they would develop all of these symptoms. Dr. Maslow found that when they followed his recommendations to "immerse themselves in something worthy of them," they usually showed a significant improvement, or the symptoms disappeared entirely. When people have worthwhile goals, life has meaning for them and the most menial tasks are possible. But when a person's work is meaningless, his life becomes meaningless as well. Closely related is what Maslow calls intellectual starvation. Intelligent people need to fufill their natural curiosity, and failure to do so can have psychopathological consequences.

Neurosis may be seen as a desperate but unsuccessful attempt by the individual to satisfy his basic needs. This point of view differs significantly from that of Freud, who saw neurosis as an attempt to satisfy unfulfilled need, but failed to distinguish between legitimate needs and illegitimate needs. Maslow points out that clinical experience shows a significant difference between filling legitimate needs and neurotic needs. The gratification of a neurotic need brings no real pleasure, but only temporary relief. The neurotic needs are "uncontrollable, inflexible, compulsive, irrational." [4] Such neurotic needs are not a part of the person's inner core, but rather an invasion of it or a defense against it. Satisfaction of neurotic needs leads to loss of capacity rather than growth.

". . . Giving gratification to neurotic needs does *not* breed health as does gratification of basic inherent needs. Giving a neurotic power-seeker all the power he wants does not make him less neurotic, nor is it possible to satiate his neurotic need for power. However much he is fed he still remains hungry. It makes little difference for ultimate health whether a neurotic need be gratified or frustrated.

"It is very different with basic needs like safety or love. Their gratification *does* breed health, their satiation *is* possible, their frustration *does* breed sickness." [1]

Lacking self-understanding, the neurotic individual tries again and again to cope with reality, but his neurotic behavior never leads to the satisfaction he seeks. The end result may be such a deep hopelessness that he simply gives up trying. Maslow believes that the apathy of the simple schizophrenic may be the expression of complete discouragement and hopelessness.

In each individual there is an inner conflict between maturity and immaturity, between responsibility and irresponsible pleasure, between impulse and control, between the desires of the individual and the demands of society. This conflict within the individual results in conflict between individuals. Problems of communication between persons are generally by-products of communication problems within the individual. As Maslow expresses it, "This pulling and hauling between individuals is paralleled by a similar conflict within each individual. The struggle between fear and courage, between defense and growth, between pathology and health is an eternal, intrapsychic struggle." [5]

Research evidence is not yet sufficient to indicate whether man's basic needs are ever completely lost. The "imprinting" experiments with chickens seem to indicate that, in a reflex system, their instincts atrophy or disappear altogether. These experiments indicate that when chickens are prevented from pecking early in life they lose the ability to peck, and the loss is apparently permanent and beyond recovery. "Perhaps," says Maslow, "infants not brought up in a loving relation in the first 18 months of life may grow up to be psychopaths, unable to love and not needing love." [6] On the other hand, he believes that, in spite of the many forces in the neurotic individual which contaminate the "wisdom of the body," it never seems to be lost altogether.

In a group of young children, classified from fully-accepted to fully-rejected, it was found that the partially rejected children behaved in a way which demonstrated their frantic need for affection, but the children who were utterly rejected from the earliest days of life exhibited, not a tremendous desire for love, but a coldness and apparent lack of desire for affection.

Psychopaths are extremely deprived individuals. "They can be described briefly as having no conscience, no guilt, no shame, no love for other people, no inhibitions, and few controls, so that they pretty well do what they want to do. They tend to become forgers, swindlers, prostitutes, polygamists, and to make their living by their wits rather than by hard work. These people because of their own lacks are generally unable to understand in others the pangs of conscience, regret, unselfish love, compassion, pity, guilt, shame, embarrassment. What you are not, you cannot perceive or understand." [7] The psychopaths are, on the other hand, extremely perceptive in discovering the psychopathic elements in others. They can spot and take advantage of a tendency toward dishonesty, greed, and phoniness, and make a living out of these weaknesses.

The basic-needs theory helps explain the behavior of some individuals who are apparently succeeding very well in the world. For example, the person who achieves political power, but seeks it for neurotic reasons, may be quite successful, but is the very type which society should watch out for because his needs for power are compulsive and never satisfied. Other individuals become very wealthy and continue to strive for more money after all their possible material needs are satisfied. Such people, though apparently successful, are actually neurotic because the accumulation of wealth alone is not satisfying; it does not satisfy the person's real but un-recognized need for respect and approval.

The basic-needs theory also clarifies another and ancient question: does sexual deprivation give rise to all of the neurotic symptoms as Freud be-lieved? Maslow writes, "It is now well known that many cases are found in which celibacy has no psychopathological effects. In many other cases, however, it has many bad effects. What factor determines which shall be the result? Clinical work with non-neurotic people gives the clear answer that sexual deprivation becomes pathogenic in a severe sense only when it is felt by the individual to represent rejection by the opposite sex, inferior-ity, lack of worth, lack of respect, isolation, or other thwarting of basic needs. Sexual deprivation can be borne with relative ease by individuals for whom it has no such implication." [1]

What Maslow has presented with his theory of basic, species-wide, un-changing psychological needs offers a clear-cut and understandable expla-nation for neurosis and psychosis, regardless of the multitudinous diversity of symptoms displayed.

Aggression

There is mounting concern in our society regarding what appears to be an increase in the incidence of violence and aggressive behavior. It is not surprising, then, that Dr. Maslow has given consideration to this special aspect of behavior or misbehavior in his comprehensive theory of human motivation.

The first point he makes is that, while there has been a great deal of discussion and theorizing, there is painfully little good solid research on the subject. Theories regarding aggression can be divided into two major categories: those who believe it is instinctual or inherited human nature, and those who believe it is not. Maslow is definitely in the second category, although he admits the evidence is not yet fully conclusive. Many behavioral scientists, Freud in particular, have considered hostility and aggressiveness as inherent in human nature. This is based on the observation that animals are aggressive and destructive; man is also an animal; thus he, too, has an instinct for violence. Maslow rejects this line of reasoning.

First, he points out that, while some animals are aggressive, many animals are not. As a matter of fact, violence and aggressiveness among members of the same species in the animal kingdom is probably more the exception than the rule. Furthermore, those species presumed to be most closely related to the human species give little evidence for an instinct of aggressiveness in the animal. This is particularly true for most of the species of monkeys which Maslow had studied and worked with in his university training. The chimpanzee, for example, evidences virtually no aggression for the sake of aggression. Maslow does aknowledge, however, that violence and aggression seem characteristic of some individual animals and some species of animals. He also refers to a study of laboratory rats, which seems to demonstrate that ferocity can be bred and passed on genetically from generation to generation.

Anthropologists have discovered that the amount of violence and hostility in primitive cultures varies from almost zero to almost one hundred percent. "There are people like the Arapesh who are so mild, so friendly, so unaggressive that they have to go to extremes to find a man who is even self-assertive enough to organize their ceremonies. At the other extreme, one can find people like the Chukchi and the Dobu who are so full of hatred that one wonders what keeps them from killing one another off altogether." [1]

Dr. Maslow's study of the Northern Blackfoot Indians convinced him that aggression was culturally rather than genetically based. He found that aggressive behavior was almost unknown to these people, although they were a proud, strong, self-reliant race. He found that even under the influence of alcohol the Indians tended to become jovial and friendly rather than aggressive.

Aggression is a reaction to the frustration of, or the inability to, satisfy basic psychological needs. It is a reaction rather than an instinct. The healthy human being who has learned to understand himself and other people will not be violent, aggressive, or destructive, although he is perfectly capable of self-defense. Healthy, mature individuals enjoy friendship, affection, cooperation, and teamwork; but neurotic and psychotic people, unable to relate with others and satisfy their powerful psychological needs for recognition and approval, find a certain pleasure in hatred and destructiveness. For individuals who perceive the world in Darwinian terms—survival of the fittest—the world is a dangerous place of dishonest, selfish, aggressive people—a jungle. For such people, aggression may be a reaction to or defense against what they perceive as a threat to themselves. The extreme in our society is the criminal psychopath, the individual who can kill, maim, or torture, apparently with complete lack of remorse. Of this individual Maslow says, "I have found it helpful in understanding psychopaths to assume that they have no love identification with other human beings and can therefore hurt them or even kill them casually without hate, and without pleasure, precisely as they kill animals who have come to be pests." [1]

Maslow assumes that since aggression is primarily cultural it generally can be prevented and cured. The evidence regarding the most serious aggression, that of criminal psychopaths, is not yet adequate. It is possible that in some cases these individuals lose their instinct for association with other humans to such an extent that it is not recoverable.

CHAPTER 9

Therapy

We have previously discussed significant theoretical differences among the three major schools of thought in psychology and psychiatry. In spite of these differences Maslow finds that satisfactory therapeutic results are obtained by all of the various clinical methods. Sometimes differences among individual therapists are more significant than differences among their theories. It becomes evident that the characteristics and abilities of the individual therapist are more important in effecting cures than his theoretical orientation.

The classical method of psychoanalysis is free association. This is the technique where the patient, in a relaxed condition, usually on a couch, talks, without too much interruption, about whatever enters his mind. The theory is that, through this apparently aimless discussion, supplemented by analysis of the patient's dreams, the patient will gain insight into the events in his past experience which have caused or are causing his difficulty. Dr. Maslow is thoroughly familiar with this methodology through his training and through personal experience as a subject of psychoanalysis. He considers this approach very helpful for some patients in recognizing and correcting some of their "infantile interpretations of self and others." [1] Dr. Maslow reports that in his early experience as a clinical psychologist he was frequently amazed to have the patient report a cure when all the doctor had done was ask questions about the problem and about the individual's life history. He tells of one instance where a college girl sought advice about a problem. After an hour, during which the student talked, and the therapist said nothing, she solved her problem to her own satisfaction and thanked the therapist profusely for his professional services.

Maslow once interviewed thirty-four individuals who had undergone various kinds of therapy within the past year. Twenty-four of them reported they were highly satisfied with their treatment and that it had helped them in a significant way. This was in spite of the fact that those interviewed had experienced a wide variety of clinical methods. It is Maslow's opinion that all the major types of psychotherapy, to the extent that they are successful, give patients insight regarding themselves, strengthen and encourage their basic instinctoid needs, and reveal, weaken, and sometimes remove altogether any neurotic needs. When therapy is successful, people change to the extent that they see things differently and think differently; their emotions and motives change; and their attitudes toward themselves and others are different. "Their characters (or personalities) change both superficially and profoundly. There is even some evidence that their appearance changes, that physical health is improved, etc. In some cases, even the IQ goes up." [1]

Sigmund Freud generally advocated a detached, impersonal relationship between the psychiatrist and his client. Now, however, more and more therapists are advocating a more personal relationship. There are vast differences in therapists, even when they are using the same methods. Maslow recommends that patient and therapist choose one another, not just on the basis of cost or reputation, but on the basis of a liking for one another. He credits Freud with the recognition that the therapist who understands himself best will be the most successful with others, and concludes that anything making the therapist a better person will also make him a better therapist. Ideally the person should be emotionally secure, financially secure in the sense that he transcends or is beyond preoccupation with money, either happily married or, at least, able to love in an enduring way, and enjoying life. For many years psychologists and psychiatrists have concentrated their attention on the most severely disturbed individuals. Now there is an increasing recognition that even the average and relatively healthy individual can be helped to gain insight about himself and become more effective in his daily living. Maslow speculates that perhaps his profession could do more for society if more time were devoted to helping healthy individuals, where a small amount of time can do a great deal of good, rather than spending long hours solely with really sick people. His personal influence and this line of reasoning has resulted in a whole series of growth centers across the nation, starting with Esalen Institute at Big Sur, California. All of these centers place their major emphasis on working to better the lives of the already-healthy rather than neurotic people.

Although he stresses the importance of trained therapists for the neurotic and psychotic, Dr. Maslow points out that, for many people, personality growth and improvement occurs with the aid of parents, teachers, ministers, good friends, good marriage partners, and sometimes just a good job. "A good marriage, success in a suitable job, developing good friendships, having children, facing emergencies and overcoming difficulties—I have occasionally seen all of these produce deep character changes, get rid of symptoms, and so forth, without the help of a technical therapist. As a matter of fact, a case could be made for the thesis that good life circumstances are among the *ultimate* therapeutic agents and that technical psychotherapy often has the task only of enabling the individual to take advantage of them." [1] A good friend with whom one can talk frankly and freely about intimate problems and worries can be tremendously helpful to psychological health.

Successful therapy, regardless of the particular method used, seems to help the patient by providing greater understanding, insight, self-knowledge, and perception of reality. This confirms the fact that mental health is almost synonymous with a good perception of reality. As people become more conscious of their own motivations, their needs, their desires, their hang-ups, they seem to develop a greater ability to solve their life problems. As people become more conscious of themselves, their solutions to life's problems become easier and require less effort. Ignorance about people reduces personal effectiveness; understanding of people increases effectiveness.

Maslow reports a general agreement among therapists regarding the importance of love to mental health. Experiments with babies have demonstrated that deprivation of love and affection early in life can lead to serious problems, even to the death of the infant. In many cases serious neuroses can be traced back to a lack of love in the early life of the individual. Fortunately, today therapists have learned to effect cures, especially for younger patients, by providing affection and kindness. In most cases this is true for adult patients, too. Successful therapy makes it possible for them to give and receive love.

Both the Freudians and the Behaviorists have contended that love is something people learn; it is not a basic instinctual characteristic in the human species. In Maslow's words, "Most theorists hold or assume that the love need is created or constructed by conditioning upon physiological-need satisfaction, e.g., that we learn to love because in the past the loved one has been a food-warmth-protection giver. This doctrine of derived needs would have to maintain then that the needs for knowledge, understanding, and beauty were acquired through conditioning upon physiological satisfaction, i.e., that they were and are signals for food, etc. Common experience supports such a contention almost not at all."[1] However, the continual evidence, especially in therapy, that the absence of love breeds emotional problems, while the presence of love and affection is basic for the healthy development of the individual, proves the instinctual nature of the love-need. Therapy can thus be seen as helping people to be more effective in their human relationship.

One of the great errors of the behavioral scientist, the psychiatrist, and the psychologist, in Maslow's opinion, is the belief that right and wrong behavior have no scientific basis. He found that therapy only succeeds to the extent that it helps people to recognize or discover better ways of behaving and thinking and relating to other people. If therapy is successful at all, it is successful because it produces better people—people who become better parents, better marriage partners, better workers, better citizens. "Professional psychotherapists every day, as a matter of course, change and improve human nature, help people to become more strong, virtuous, creative, kind, loving, altruistic, serene. These are only some of the consequences of improved self-knowledge and self-acceptance."[2]

Insight therapy works because it helps the individual to uncover himself, to discover within himself the need for right behavior, to discover the truth about himself. Gratification of the basic needs requires the ability to relate to other people. Unless interpersonal skills are increased, the patient will have difficulty satisfying his needs for safety, belongingness, love, and respect. This is also true, although to a lesser extent, for satisfying the needs for self-respect, knowledge, and understanding. The successful therapist must help the individual to a greater ability to satisfy the basic needs, and, thus, move the individual up the path toward self-actualization. This Maslow defines as the "ultimate goal of all therapy." [1]

Dr. Maslow was successful in producing a marked increase in the self-esteem of a very shy and retiring woman by the following technique: she was instructed to assert herself in twenty specific but rather trivial situations. For example, she was to insist that her grocer obtain a certain product for her and disregard his objections. Within three months it was evident that her self-esteem had improved enough to change her general behavior. She was able to wear form-fitting clothing, which she had previously avoided. For the first time she was able to wear and appear in public in a swim suit, something she had previously been too bashful to do. Her husband reported an improvement in her sexual behavior which had previously been badly inhibited. The content of her dreams changed, and she was able to handle a number of situations which had previously seemed too difficult.

If self-understanding is the key to mental health, why does the typical patient in therapy seem to resist recognition of truth? Maslow explains that it is a natural tendency to protect the self-image—one's ego. Furthermore, reality can be very threatening, especially to the insecure person.

Some people who are generally secure are still troubled by specific fears. Maslow found that such fears are usually the result of some specific conditioning experience and that, for this type of problem, Behavioristic reconditioning treatment is very successful. For such people, what Maslow calls simple reconditioning—intellectual explanation, encouragement to strengthen the will power, and exhortation—is sufficient, but these same methods are completely useless for a *really* insecure person. From this he concludes, "We might say that the fear that is inconsistent with the rest of the personality is easily removed; the fear that is consistent with the rest of the personality is very tenacious." [1]

As has been dicussed, many therapists believe that guilt is an important cause of neurosis. Their solution is to convince the patient that his guilt is the unnecessary result of a puritanical training. But Maslow believes real guilt is the result of a person's failure to live up to his own potential. When this condition exists, the therapists must help the patient to identify and recognize the reason for his guilty feeling. ". . . the implication is very clear that we are going to be less tolerant, less relative about these things, and more judgmental." [3] Psychologists are now recognizing that there is a healthy unconscious as well as an unhealthy one. It is the healthy unconscious which needs to be revealed and strengthened.

The authoritarian personality who perceives the world as dangerous may not respond well to the therapist who seems gentle and trusting; for such individuals a stern, strict approach may be best. To treat them by offering freedom and trust actually increases their bad behavior. Similarly, the deeply dependent and passive individual cannot accept sudden freedom and responsibility. "The big point here is not to think that good conditions inevitably make all human beings into growing, self-actualizing people. Certain forms of neurosis don't respond in this way." [3]

During the summer of 1962 when Abraham Maslow was a visiting Fellow at Western Behavioral Science and Nonlinear Systems he was invited by Dr. Robert Tannenbaum to visit one of the UCLA sensitivity training groups at Lake Arrowhead. This was his first exposure to one of these training groups (T-groups, as they are called); he had not even read very much about them. It was a new and exciting experience. Steeped in the method of psychoanalysis, he was impressed both by the similarities and by the differences between analysis and T-groups. Sensitivity training is unstructured: that is, a group of people are brought together, but are given almost no instructions. They just sit and talk to and about each other. This is similar to the psychoanalytic technique of encouraging the subject to ramble, to say whatever comes into his head. The sensitivity training group has almost no agenda and, it seems to many of the participants at first, no purpose. The technique is very similar to Carl Rogers' non-directive type of therapy. Maslow also related it to Taoistic philosophy of "non-interference—letting things happen of their own accord and in their own style." [3] Maslow had used a similar approach in the graduate department of Brandeis. "I learned with my Taoistic and permissive graduate department of psychology at Brandeis that lack of structuring and permissiveness provides the very best atmosphere to encourage the deepest psychic strengths, self-actualizing tendencies to emerge in the open;

but I also learned that this same lack of structure in the department could bring to the surface all the weaknesses in the person—the lack of talent, the blocks and inhibitions, and so on. That is, the unstructured situation tended either to make or break them; many turned out either marvelously well or else failed altogether." [3]

The T-group he observed was composed of businessmen, engineers, corporate executives—men who were practical, hard-headed, and probably in better than average psychological health. Psychoanalysts generally expect to spend two or three years—several hours each week—to solve a patient's problem. Maslow was astonished at the rapidity with which these group participants learned free association and how to express their hostilities and innermost feelings. He saw the tremendous possibilities for both healthy and psychologically unhealthy individuals to speed the process that was so slow and expensive under the older, traditional methods. "These people behaved and talked in a spontaneous and free way that I have ordinarily associated with psychoanalyzed people, that is, with people who have been under psychoanalysis for a year or two at least. I have always assumed, I think without quite realizing it, the psychoanalytic point of view that any change in character is going to take two or three years to make. Well, apparently it can happen a lot faster, *very* much faster in this kind of social situation." [3]

Not only did the T-group method offer valuable shortcuts to the psychoanalytical method, but something was happening in the T-group that might not occur in non-group situations. Maslow speculated that a combination of group and individual therapy would be very effective. In the T-group things happened and happened fast. Maslow suspected that one of the reasons was that the type of people participating were "thing" people who had never before been exposed to self-analysis. These people quickly learned to examine their own feelings and motives; they became aware of other people in a psychic way: aware of their feelings and emotions and aware of the difficulty of communicating these things. It was the type of experience that forced them to examine assumptions and mannerisms which had become an integral part of their personalities. These men found that honest, productive criticism, instead of building animosities, frequently built mutual respect and affection for one another. The participants were learning to be more realistic and objective, to be more aware of emotions, and to be tolerant of them. "Another approach to this whole business is to call it honesty training or spontaneity training . . . or another phrase that maybe sums it all up . . . is intimacy training, the strong impression I got so often was of people struggling to drop their defenses, their guards, and their masks as they got less afraid of being hurt. . . . The learning to tolerate the lack of structure, ambiguity, planlessness, the lack of future, the lack of predictability, the lack of control of the future, all this is extremely therapeutic and psychologic." [3]

Psychoanalysts have always maintained that personality change required probing into the past, that psychological problems are deeply rooted in the unconscious mind. Sensitivity training challenges this, dealing as it does with the present and the future. It was apparent to Maslow that the group experience changed peoples' attitudes and behavior, actually changed their personalities, and these changes were being obtained without "probing into the history of the person, into the origins of his neurotic attitudes. . . . psychoanalysts have assumed that the main determinant of behavior lay hidden deeply within the person, i.e., that it was intrapersonal rather than social or interpersonal. These group people are showing that we had better lay a great deal more stress on the current social interpersonal situation as a determinant of interpersonal behavior and even of self-awareness." [3] Dr. Maslow was excited about the social implications of what he saw, seeing a possible method for improving people and improving society, and a fairly economical way to change individuals and groups of individuals and improve human relations, thus creating a better world.

CHAPTER 10

Values

"The ultimate disease of our times is valuelessness . . . this state is more crucially dangerous than ever before in history; and . . . something can be done about it by man's own effort." [1]

Perhaps the most unique aspect of Maslow's Third Force theory is the belief that there are values or moral principles common to the entire human species, which can be scientifically confirmed. Maslow strongly feels the need for a usable system of values that does not rest upon blind faith alone. "It is certainly true that mankind, throughout history, has looked for guiding values, for principles of right and wrong. But he has tended to look outside of himself, outside of mankind to a god, to some sort of sacred book perhaps, or to a ruling class. What I am doing is to explore the theory that you can find the values by which mankind must live, and for which man has always sought, by digging into the best people in depth. I believe, in other words, that I can find ultimate values which are right for mankind by observing the best of mankind. If under the best conditions and in the best specimens I simply stand aside and describe in a scientific way what these human values are. I find values that are the old values of truth, goodness, and beauty, and some additional ones as well—for instance, gaiety, justice, and joy." [2] They are intrinsic in human nature, a part of man's biological nature, instinctual rather than acquired.

Maslow feels that, with a scientific approach to values, the Third Force psychologist can solve human problems that have plagued man for centuries. "For one thing," he says, "it looks as if there were a single ultimate value for mankind, a far goal toward which all men strive. This is called variously by different authors, self-actualization, self-realization, integration, psychological health, individuation, autonomy, creativity, productivity, but they all agree that this amounts to realizing the potentialities of the person, that is to say, becoming fully human, everything that the person can become." [3]

Maslow objects vehemently to the idea that the study of human behavior must ignore all concepts of right and wrong. This point of view stems directly from the Behavioristic assumption that values have no scientific basis. Maslow believes that, if behavioral scientists are to solve human problems, the question of right and wrong behavior is essential—the very essence of behavioral science. Psychologists who advocate moral and cultural relativism (and the majority do) are not coming to grips with the real problems of our society. On the assumption that all higher needs or higher forms of behavior are learned and have no genetic basis, behavioral scientists have rejected not only the methods of religion but the values as well. This point of view does not fit with the observable facts. Maslow says, "The casting out of values by psychology not only weakens it, and prevents it from reaching its full growth, but also abandons mankind either to supernaturalism or to ethical relativism." [4]

For example, a man like Adolf Eichmann cannot be explained by a Behavioristic, relativistic theory of behavior. As far as Eichmann was concerned, everything was fine; he did a good job; he was most efficient. This exemplifies the very danger of value-free science. Without ethical ends, a society must expect men like Eichmann and Hitler, and atom bombs, and the like.

In Maslow's words, "Instead of cultural relativity, I am implying that there are basic, underlying, human standards that are cross-cultural—which transcend cultures and which are broadly human. Without these standards we simply would have no criterion for criticizing, let us say, the well-adjusted Nazi in Nazi Germany." [2]

So the free choices of self-actualizing people, healthy people, normal people, tell us what is good and what is bad, and this is the basis for a naturalistic value system. When we separate the healthy specimens from the rest of the population and determine what they struggle toward, seek, desire, as they grow and improve themselves, and what values are lacking among those who are psychologically sick, we have an understanding of right and wrong. And this can be scientifically validated. Thus man's higher aspirations, his ideals, and his spiritual life are proper subjects for scientific research because they are biologically based. The mistake that has been frequently made in the past is to average the values of healthy and sick people, of good and bad choosers. "Only the choices and tastes and judgments of healthy human beings will tell us much about what is good for the human species in the long run." [3] The choices of self-actualizers seem to be essentially the same around the world, indicating that the basic needs are universal and cross-cultural.

The concept of common species-wide values, however, must also allow for some variations in human needs. Psychologists cannot ignore the fact that people have different capacities—mental, physical, dietary, etc.—and to the extent these capacities vary, people's needs vary, too.

There is a scientific basis for responsible behavior, and, in the final analysis, irresponsibility is just as damaging to the individual as to his society. As Maslow succinctly put it, "Time wounds all heels." Thus, many crimes against society are crimes against one's own nature and, as such, record themselves in the unconscious and make us despise ourselves. Either people do things which are fine and good and, thus, respect themselves, or they do contemptible things and feel despicable, worthless, and unlovable. This point of view is similar to that of Socrates: the man with full knowledge would never do evil because the fully enlightened man would recognize the damaging effects upon himself. Thus Maslow states, . . . "ignorance of the facts is a major source of evil behavior. . . . The whole of Jeffersonian democratic theory is based on the conviction that full knowledge leads to right action, and that right action is impossible without full knowledge." [5]

"Throughout history, learned men have set out before mankind the rewards of virtue, the beauties of goodness, the intrinsic desirability of psychological health and self-fulfilment. It's all as plain as A, B, C, yet most people perversely refuse to step into the happiness and self-respect that is offered them." [6] Saints and prophets have talked of these higher values for thousands of years, but one of the problems has been that their revelations have not always been accurate. There is the need for a scientific method of checking the validity of subjective conclusions. "Too many visionaries, seers, and prophets have turned out to be incorrect after *feeling* absolutely certain." [5]

Organized religions have sometimes made the mistake of concentrating on the higher values alone, rather than starting with the lower needs for food, shelter, and clothing, which, says Maslow, are more basic than sermons. Many religions have tended to emphasize man's worst aspects as intrinsic, but have failed to recognize that higher values are intrinsic, too.

Behaviorists put great stress on cultural influence. Carried to the extreme, this means that the individual is the captive of his culture and cannot break away from it. This, Maslow points out, is only true for the weaker members of the human race. Self-actualizers are influenced far more by their understanding of themselves and their own basic needs than by cultural values, which may or may not be genuine. Thus it is possible for individuals to be healthier than the culture surrounding them.

As mentioned earlier, Maslow calls the higher, or ultimate values sought by self-actualizing adults Being-values or B-values. Following once more, is the list of B-values which he heard again and again from self-actualizing people and from other people as a result of their peak experiences: "Truth, beauty, wholeness, dichotomy-transcendence (transformation of opposites into unities, of antagonists into collaborating or mutually enhancing partners), aliveness, uniqueness, perfection, necessity, completion, justice, order, simplicity, richness, effortlessness, playfulness, self-sufficiency." [1] The self-actualizing person incorporates these values into himself, so that attacks upon these values are treated the same as attacks upon himself. Maslow found that these values are so interrelated that they must be used to define one another. "For instance, truth was beautiful, truth was good, truth was just, truth was final, truth was perfect, truth was complete, truth was unitary, truth was rich, and so on for the whole list of B-values." [7]

Value-illness or neurosis or psychopathology may be called anhedonia, anomie, apathy, amorality, hopelessness, cynicism, etc.—conditions, which can lead to physical illness as well. Maslow believes the cure for valuelessness is obvious: the development of a validated usable system of human values that people can prove to themselves and believe in because it is biologically true. "The state of being without a system of values is psycho-pathogenic. Human beings need a philosophy of life, religion, or a value system, just as they need sunlight, calcium and love." [3] The person who lacks a value system may be impulsive, nihilistic, totally skeptic; in other words, his life is meaningless.

If good behavior is natural to man, why is bad behavior so prevalent? The answer in part, has been dealt with, before—man's instincts are weak and easily misunderstood or ignored, and are frequently weaker than cultural forces. Also, there is the aforementioned dichotomy of the simultaneous presence of an innate drive toward growth and an innate tendency to retreat toward safety.

So, in essence, it can be seen that all human beings must have a value system. And Maslow's work and that of others have demonstrated that such a value system exists. In a recent interview Dr. Maslow spoke of the so-called generation gap, expressing sadness that youngsters, radical youngsters and hippies in particular, are searching so hard for truth, honesty, beauty, and brotherhood. "And I would say to them, for the love of Pete it is already existing. You are searching for some kind of future and it is here and it is now. All you have to do is turn to it." [8]

CHAPTER **II**

Eupsychian
Management

In the summer of 1962 Abraham Maslow became what he termed a "sort of visiting fellow" at Non-Linear Systems, Inc., a digital voltmeter factory in the little town of Del Mar, California.

"I came there for no specific task or purpose," Dr. Maslow stated, "but I became very much interested in what was going on there for various reasons." [1] It was the first time he had been exposed to enlightened, modern management in a business firm. He began to take notes each night, dictating into a tape machine. The transcriptions of his tapes became a personal, informal journal, which eventually became his book, *Eupsychian Management*.

This book was not merely an attempt to describe what was going on at Non-Linear; it comprised his ideas and thoughts about people and their organizations as he observed, studied, and made his notes.

He saw industry as "a source of knowledge, replacing the laboratory, often far more useful than the laboratory . . . a new kind of life laboratory with going-on researches where I can confidently expect to learn much about standard problems of classical psychology, e.g., learning, motivation, emotion, thinking, acting, etc." [1]

In addition to his observations Maslow read voraciously in this "fascinating new field of social psychology." He read Peter Drucker's *Principles of Management*[2] and Douglas MacGregor's *The Human Side of Enterprise*[3], both of which were considered texts at Non-Linear.

Maslow was impressed with the fact that Peter Drucker, a management consultant, had reached conclusions about human nature that were very similar to his own, purely by observing industrial and management situations. Apparently Drucker and other management consultants had taken a look at "what passes for scientific psychology" and had given it up as having little value. Maslow thought it was unfortunate that, while throwing out some of the less-useful conclusions from experiments with rats, pigeons, and conditioned reflex, the management consultants had thrown out some nuggets as well.

Understandably, Maslow was particularly interested in Douglas MacGregor's book, since it described management theories which were based primarily on Maslow's own theories of basic needs.

MacGregor took issue with what he termed "Theory X Management," which was basically authoritarian and the commonest form of management in the business world. This theory assumes that the average human being dislikes work, and because of this he must be coerced, controlled, directed, and even threatened by punishment in order to get the job done.

MacGregor then described "Theory Y Management," which is based on Maslow's thinking and makes the following assumptions:

"1. The expenditure of physical and mental effort in work is as natural as play or rest. The average human being does not inherently dislike work. Depending upon controllable conditions, work may be a source of satisfaction (and will be voluntarily performed) or a source of punishment (and will be avoided if possible).

2. External control and the threat of punishment are not the only means for bringing about effort toward organizational objectives. Man will exercise self-direction and self-control in the service of objectives to which he is committed.

3. Commitment to objectives is a function of the rewards associated with their achievement. The most significant of such rewards, e.g. the satisfaction of ego and self-actualization needs, can be direct products of effort directed toward organizational objectives.

4. The average human being learns, under proper conditions, not only to accept but to seek responsibility.

5. The capacity to exercise a relatively high degree of imagination, ingenuity, and creativity in the solution of organizational problems is widely, not narrowly, distributed in the population.

6. Under the conditions of modern industrial life, the intellectual potentialities of the average human being are only partially utilized." [3]

While generally excited about and convinced of the practicality of Theory Y Management, Maslow saw that the positive approach, allowing workers to see their interests as being synonymous with the interests of their organization, would not work with overly insecure, untrusting types of people. His feeling was that MacGregor had insufficient understanding of this type of person; thus, Theory Y Management depended upon starting with generally well-adjusted people. Maslow said, "Given fairly okay people to begin with, in a fairly good organization, then work tends to improve people. This tends to improve the industry, which in turn tends to improve the people involved, and so it goes . . . proper management of the work lives of human beings, in the way in which they earn their living, can improve them and improve the world and in this sense be a Utopian or revolutionary technique." [1]

For example, a Theory Y type of system would certainly not work in a country inhabited by fearful people. Under this condition, strong leadership is not only best, it is necessary—just as it is in certain situations, such as war, where prompt, unquestioned orders must be given and obeyed. Maslow stated, "The tough and hard, but capable leader may be hated, but he is much preferred to the soft and tender weak leader who may be more lovable, but who may also bring about one's death. There are still plenty of people, even in the U.S., and certainly in many other countries of the world, who are frightened to death, who much prefer to be dependent and slavish and who don't want to make up their own minds. . . . There are many places in the world where only authoritarian management, cracking the whip over fearful people, can work. For example, Columbia, Iran, Syria, and South Africa." [1]

He also referred to studies of the German character during World War II, which indicated that the Germans expected leaders, professors, teachers, managers, and foremen to be tough, stern, and harsh.

Elaborating on the subject of work, Maslow said that healthy people prefer work to idleness, but that most people will prefer no work to meaningless, worthless, or wasted work. Maslow recalls a patient, a woman, who was depressed and had lost her zest for life because she was personnel manager in a chewing gum factory and considered chewing gum of no constructive value in the world. However, for the man who likes his job and considers it worthwhile, work is an enjoyable part of life. This observation conforms to Maslow's theory of basic needs—the idea that healthy people have a need to work, to grow, to achieve, to be worthwhile.

Another healthy aspect of the work situation, frequently overlooked by other theorists, is the pleasure of being one of a team, working cooperatively with others as part of a well-organized, well-functioning organization. Again, this is true for the healthy person; but for the deeply disturbed person, there are instances when the pleasure of hatred and destruction is greater than the pleasure of friendship and cooperation. With only one qualification—healthy workers—Theory Y Management will be more productive in the long run than Theory X. Not only can Theory Y produce a better society, but in a practical hardheaded way, it is the path to industrial and financial success.

In dealing with Theories "X" and "Y" it is important to remember that when workers have been used to tough, centralized, authoritarian management, any transition to a more enlightened participative type of management should be done gradually. Some workers are apt to take advantage of what they consider the weakness of managers.

Maslow learned this from first-hand experience in the classroom. Some students were used to being dictated to and thought anything else was soft-headed and tried to take advantage. With these types Maslow found it best to be tough, to crack down, to make it very clear he was the boss. After they fully recognized his authority, he gradually was able to show them that one could be in charge without being constantly dictatorial.

One reason Theory Y management works better than Theory X is that dictatorial management injures the dignity and self-respect of the worker, who, consciously or unconsciously, fights back to protect his own self-esteem and self-respect. The result may be hostility toward management, vandalism, or malingering. Maslow reiterates what most good managers have learned the hard way: approval and recognition build the worker's self-esteem and spur him to greater productivity.

Not only does this understanding of people's need for self-esteem have tremendous significance in the field of management, but the principle has great significance in understanding minority groups and others held in low self-esteem. For example, there was an era, described in Turkish and Arabic literature, when women were treated as nothing, with neither dignity nor respect; their behavior was very similar to that of Negro slaves in the South before the Civil War. These women did not dare to retaliate openly, but found sly, secretive methods of "getting even." Maslow's point is that such types of reaction to injustice actually confirm the dignity of man rather his degradation. "A neurosis can be seen either as a sign of sin and evil and human weakness and degradation on the one hand, or can be seen with deeper understanding and insight, as a frightened person's indirect struggle toward health, growth, and self-actualization. The whole of the foregoing is applicable to the response of the worker in a bad industrial situation; he may show his anger at being dehumanized in all sorts of sneaky ways, but these are essentially testimonials to his fear rather than to his lack of growth possibilities." [1]

Practically all research in the industrial situation supports Theory Y, and practically none of it, Theory X. An obvious point to be learned from this, Maslow feels, is that industry needs a steady supply of mature, well-adjusted people. Industry will have trouble, he points out, using delinquents, criminals, cynical kids, or hostile, destructive people. Today such types are being used, but their use will be successful only when attitudes are changed.

For industry to be successful, healthy managers are as important as healthy workers. The psychologically healthy manager not only will get more production from his workers, he will increase their psychological health as well. Thus, "The better man and the better group are the causes and effects of each other and the better group and the better society are the causes and effects of each other. . ." [1]

Corroborating this point, Dr. Maslow has cited the studies of Rensis Likert. Strangely enough, Dr. Likert found that, in the organization where there is more participation in management throughout the company, the men at the top actually have more influence rather than less. "That is, the more influence and power you give to someone else in the team situation, the more you have to yourself." [1]

This brings us to the concept of power. Many people assume that power in the form of strong leadership is always bad, overlooking the fact that there are healthy leaders whose motives are for the good of their organization and the good of society. It is incorrect to assume that all leadership is an unhealthy hunger for selfish power. The key words thus are *healthy* and *unhealthy*. So, good or bad leadership depends to a large degree on whether or not the leader is psychologically healthy or unhealthy.

Another important aspect of leadership is that a given leader should not let himself become too sensitive to the feelings of his followers. "The kind of person," says Maslow, "who must be loved by all probably will not make a good leader." [1] There are times when the leader must say no, be tough, strong, and courageous. Thus, the leader with high self-esteem can have the courage to withstand expedient demands which might be damaging to the organization in the long run. The really excellent boss is the one who takes pleasure in seeing his workers grow and self-actualize.

Dr. Maslow points out that Theory Y management calls for a more trusting, open, participative type of organization. However, a realistic understanding that there are some people who cannot be trusted is also necessary. If the manager is not realistic about people, Theory Y can get him into trouble. There can also be a problem if the leader is so vastly superior to those around him that participative management is difficult and frustrating for him. Such a leader quickly sees what should be done while all the others are struggling slowly. Under these conditions, keeping his mouth shut can be physical torture. Such a person in such a situation will naturally tend toward more authoritative leadership.

Maslow feels that our society generally has tended to underrate the importance of the entrepreneur. "The most valuable one hundred people to bring into a deteriorating society, like, for instance, Peru, would not be one hundred chemists or politicians or professors or engineers, but rather one hundred entrepreneurs." [1] A good entrepreneur may be worth huge sums of money to his society, but it is also true that great differences in income breed envy and jealousy. Maslow speculates that we should find ways other than money to reward entrepreneurs. In the Eupsychian Society it is important that cream rise to the top. "The best product should be bought, the best man should be rewarded more. Interfering factors which befuddle the triumph of virtue, justice, truth, and efficiency, etc., should be kept to an absolute minimum, or should approach zero as a limit. . . . Any determinant that increases the health of a particular person, making him therefore not only a better manager or better worker or better citizen, but also a better consumer, must be considered to be good for the health of any particular enterprise. . . . If swindling pays, then it will not stop. The definition of the good society is one in which virtue pays." In fact, he puts it even more emphatically: "You cannot have a good society unless virtue pays." [1]

Thus, we can see that Eupsychian management applies to a larger scope than industry—to society, in general. A healthy functioning society needs followers who have the ability to recognize and admire superiority and choose superior people as leaders. In the ideal society, Maslow states, "success and wealth of any kind and status would then be perfectly correlated with actual capacity and skill and talent." [1]

There can be found in society situations where there are so many fearful, indecisive, insecure people that a strong, powerful leader, even if he is the wrong kind of leader, will find many followers. Hitler and Stalin are examples of this.

Applying this subject to nations Maslow asks: even if we can avoid a shooting war, who will win the cold war? The answer, he believes, is the nation that turns out the best type of individual—healthy, strong, enthusiastic, and creative.

The more Maslow studied the industrial situation at Non-Linear and the supporting literature, the more he became convinced of its essential soundness. "This is no longer quite a theory," he said, "but it is rather a fact." [1] There is empirical evidence to confirm Theory Y for most American citizens, and there is empirical evidence to disconfirm Theory X for most American citizens.

Never guilty of oversimplification, Maslow points out that we should not make the mistake of thinking that good working conditions will automatically make all people into better, growing, self-actualizing people. Some forms of neurosis simply don't respond to this kind of treatment. "Freedom and trust given to authoritarians, for instance, will simply bring out bad behavior in these people. Freedom and permissiveness and responsibility will make really dependent and passive people collapse in anxiety and fear." [1]

He says that we should not make the mistake of thinking that most existing American Corporations are badly managed; there is a tremendous variation between reasonably good companies and some small businesses in highly competitive cut-throat fields, where the manager can only survive by bleeding all he can out of his employees. Compared to other parts of the world, even America's worst is not so bad. "Ninety-nine percent of the human species would give several years of their lives to get a job in the worst-managed large corporation we have in the whole country." [1]

Maslow concludes that the pressure of competition will gradually and steadily move American management toward Theory Y. "Old style management is steadily becoming obsolete, putting the enterprise in a less and less advantageous position in competition with other enterprises in the same industry that are under enlightened management and are, therefore, turning out better products, better services, etc." [1]

CHAPTER 12

The Third Force
and Social Reform

"When the philosophy of man (his nature, his goals, his potentialities, his fulfillment) changes, then everything changes; not only the philosophy of politics, economics, of ethics, of values, of interpersonal relations, and of history itself, but also the philosophy of education, the theory of how to help men become what they can and deeply need to become.

"We are now in the middle of such a change in the conception of man's capacities, potentialities, and goals. A new vision is emerging of the possibilities of man and his destiny, and its implications are many, . . ." [1]

Clearly, the comprehensive theory of behavior and motivation advanced by Dr. Abraham Maslow challenges the whole edifice of western intellectual thought, which, in the last four or five decades, has leaned so heavily on the theories of Sigmund Freud and John B. Watson and other Behaviorists. These deterministic theories have stressed the need for laws, controls, regulations, and prohibitions. What Maslow is suggesting is a more positive view of man and his potential and greater emphasis on discovering, developing, uncovering, and releasing man's higher nature.

In the self-actualizing person, the person who is moving or growing in a healthy way, the lower needs are not at war with the higher needs. "Most civilizations," says Maslow, "along with their theories of politics, education, religion, etc., have been based on the exact contradictory of this belief. On the whole, they have assumed the primitive, animal, and instinctive aspects of human nature to be severely limited to the physiological needs for food, sex and the like. The higher impulses for truth, for love, for beauty were assumed to be intrinsically different in nature from these animal needs. Furthermore these interests were assumed to be antagonistic, mutually exclusive, and in perpetual conflict with each other for mastery." [2]

The identification of basic needs common to the entire human species encourages far more optimism for cross-cultural harmony than most people now believe. In the study of self-actualizing people Maslow found their similarities far greater than their differences, regardless of their cultural heritage. He found such concepts as freedom, love, justice, and beauty to be universal in superior individuals. Behavioral scientists who believe man is merely another species of animal, and make the prior assumption that animals are primarily selfish, see man as constantly in conflict with his society. Freud was particularly vehement about this point. To Maslow this is true only for the ignorant, immature, or neurotic individual. The healthy individual's selfish interests and the interests of society become synonymous. This point of view is very similaar to that of Adam Smith, *Wealth of Nations*, 1776, whose "enlightened man" advanced the interest of society in the intelligent pursuit of his own self-interest. (A point of view, incidentally, which was very influential, probably dominant, in the minds of the men who wrote the Declaration of Independence.) The individual who recognizes and seeks to gratify his higher needs behaves voluntarily in a manner beneficial to his society. A person who receives love and respect must of necessity behave in a respectable way. "People who have enough basic satisfaction to look for love and respect (rather than just food and safety) tend to develop such qualities as loyalty, friendliness, and civic consciousness, and to become better parents, husbands, teachers, public servants, etc. . . . To accept as intrinsic an antagonism between instincts and society, between individual interests and social interests was a

terrific begging of the question. Possibly its main excuse was that in the
sick society and in the sick individual, it actually tends to be true. Individual and social interests under healthy social conditions are synergic and
not antagonistic." [2]

The better society is the society which provides an environment encouraging the development of man's potential. Some basic elements of this
external environment—what Maslow calls the preconditions for need-
satisfaction—are freedom, justice, and order. Our present society has
placed far too much emphasis on material and economic success, and too
little on human, psychological, and spiritual success. The good society encourages and permits the satisfaction of man's psychological needs while
the bad society frustrates need-satisfaction. What Maslow describes as a
psychologically sick society, has "not enough love, affection, protection,
respect, trust, and too much hostility, humiliation, fear, contempt, and
domination." [2]

Because man's psychological needs are weak and easily frustrated,
many individuals, perhaps the majority, are not able to rise above a bad
culture. A healthy culture, in Maslow's opinion, would significantly reduce
the need for psychotherapy; there would not be as much mental illness if
we had a better society. The necessary ingredients for the good society
can be scientifically determined through the study of human motivation.
The factors are built into human nature and cannot be voted out of existence. Maslow compares this to the gardener who can help a rose bush to
grow but cannot make it become an oak tree. A healthy society would
reward virtue and fail to reward evil—a society, as he put it, where "the
cream rises to the top." Maslow observed that in a society where truth is
distorted or withheld, the effects on the society are very negative, leading
to distrust, cynicism, suspicion, and poor interpersonal relationships.

Abraham Maslow set out in 1941 to find a comprehensive theory of
human motivation which would contribute significantly to a better society.
He was sickened by what he saw going on in Europe during World War
II. In his book, *Eupsychian Management* (1965), he discusses the application of Third Force theory to social betterment. The process that he envisions is a slow, gradual, nonviolent, steady improvement in society. Society must be understood as an integrated whole, with each part related to
the other parts, each change affecting the whole, at least to some degree.
To improve society we must improve all of the institutions, although not

necessarily simultaneously. By improving society we improve individuals, by improving individuals we improve society. The effective reformer is one who is willing to work hard, with dedication and discipline, even at a relatively small task.

The trouble with many young people today, Maslow believes, is that they want some sudden improvement in the world, but are not willing to work at it. They become discouraged by the immensity of our social problems and the apparent hopelessness of the individual effecting them. "This is the real danger that I see, especially in our younger people in the teens and twenties and thirties, that they feel helpless in the face of atom bombs and huge international conferences and cold wars and the like. They are then apt to turn to a truly selfish and private life. . . . Colin Wilson talks about the choice between being a hero or a worm; so many choose wormhood."[3] Discovering better and more effective ways toward personal growth and self-actualization are important aspects of social reform.

Too many people have interpreted Third Force theory in a passive, indulgent manner. They want to wait until inspiration strikes them or they have a peak experience. They believe that life should be always enjoyable. "More dependent, more indulged, more oral, more passive people are interpreting this philosophy of self-actualization to mean 'waiting for inspiration,' waiting for something to happen, waiting for something to grab them, waiting for some peak experience which will tell them automatically and without effort what their destiny is and what they should do. Part of this feeling of self-indulgence is that anything which is self-actualizing should be enjoyable. . . . Cultivating one's capacities can be hard work, . . . (even though it may simultaneously be enjoyed). . . ."[3]

We should stop looking for one single Utopian answer and concentrate on constant steady improvement, one step at a time. There's no reason we couldn't conduct several experimental approaches simultaneously to find out which is best. The job is too big for any one person. It requires many people working in many different areas. If our society had some common goals, more people could become involved. Enlightened business managers are discovering that their organizations are most effective when there are common goals that everyone knows, understands, and contributes toward. Maslow sees private industry as a powerful and important sector of society. Enlightened managers can help their employees to grow, to become better citizens, and this can contribute significantly to improvement of the entire society. Improving the world by changing people in individual therapy is obviously not going to do the job . . . "Individual psychoanalysis is absolutely of no use in changing the world by changing people one by one." [3]

Maslow is critical of the "life adjustment approach." In this approach, which the Behaviorists have popularized, psychological health is seen as learning to adjust to society rather than adjusting society to conform with our species-wide needs. Trying to help people adjust to a mediocre society is not the path to social reform. Such a philosophy seems related to that of Karl Marx: "As I understand Marxist psychology, it also is a very blunt and unmistakable expression of the view that the psyche is a mirror to reality. . . . For a theory of mental health," Maslow suggests, "extra-psychic success is not enough; we must also include intra-psychic health." [1]

Education is obviously an important force for or against social improvement. In Third Force theory education may be described as "good" if it helps the individual to develop his potential, helps him toward self-actualization. Present day education, in Maslow's opinion, falls far short of what is needed. He says bluntly, "Our conventional education looks mighty sick." [4] He asks why so much of educational psychology concerns itself with means—grades, degrees, credits, and diplomas—rather than such ends as wisdom, understanding, and good judgment. "Part of the job of teaching," he said, "is to teach that big, noble-sounding, resounding words like patriotism and democracy and social betterment and the like translate themselves down into the hour-to-hour, day-to-day slugging away at tasks which are means to the end." [3]

Society needs to learn to identify those best qualified for leadership. There has been too much suspicion of leadership—not all are power-hungry and dangerous. There are leaders who see their role as a necessary service to society. As an example, Maslow says, "It is quite clear that Jefferson never wanted power or leadership for any selfish benefits that might come from it, but that he felt rather that he should sacrifice himself because he could do a good job that needed to be done." [2] There has been a tendency to place too much emphasis on all men being equal. Even management literature seems to avoid carefully the idea that perhaps some men are better qualified for leadership than others. We need to learn to identify and respect leaders, rather than treating them with suspicion, envy, and even dislike.

Dr. Maslow was very much impressed with the Blackfeet Indians' choice of leaders. The Indians always chose the man best qualified for a particular job. If it were a building project, they picked the best builder as leader. If it were a hunting party, they picked a hunter, and so forth. They knew from experience just the right man for each specific leadership situation.

In the good society success and ability should be closely correlated. "As a matter of fact that's the way we could define a good society if we wanted to, as one in which all those who are on top deserve to be there; or those who were elected to high office were the very best persons in the society; and those who were the best people in the society were necessarily elected to the highest offices."[3] We need to develop people with the courage to lead, the courage to be sparkplugs, the courage to disagree. In Maslow's opinion, America has too many meek, mild, appeasing men who avoid all disagreements or compromise too willingly or give in too easily to the majority. The great leader is one who has just the right combination of humility and flexibility and, at the same time, the strength of character to stand alone when an important principle is involved.

Economists both East and West have almost totally ignored the higher needs. Almost all economic theory is too materialistic. "We must say harshly of the 'science' of economics that it is generally the skilled, exact, technological application of a totally false theory of human needs and values, a theory which recognizes only the existence of lower needs or material needs."[5]

The quality of society is very important to industry. A healthy society breeds healthy industry, and conversely, a healthy industry breeds a healthier society. He cites Japan as an example where the increasing quality of the product improves society because it increases Japanese self-esteem. The business community needs healthy people and cannot flourish indefinitely in an environment of riot, civil war, violence, or political corruption. Too much political interference is bad for healthy industry. Autocratic leadership stifles rather than encourages self-actualization. When all of the decisions are made by leadership, people become more and more dependent, and less and less able to make their own decisions. Industry is becoming aware of this situation and is doing something about it. We need to consider this in our political policies as well. If we can avoid a nuclear holocaust, and Maslow is optimistic about this because he believes we have achieved a balance of power stalemate, Third Force theory offers considerable hope for the future. If the entire human species has common basic needs, which, when developed, are social rather than anti-social, the long-range prognosis for the human species is far more optimistic than that projected by Freud or Marx.

"We can now reject, as a localism, the almost universal mistake that the interests of the individual and of society are of necessity mutually exclusive and antagonistic, or that civilization is primarily a mechanism for controlling and policing human instinctoid impulses. All these age-old axioms are swept away by the new possibility of defining the main function of a healthy culture as the fostering of universal self-actualization." [1]

CHAPTER 13

The Synergic Society

Dr. Maslow got the word and the idea for the synergic society from Ruth Benedict (1887–1948), a professor of anthropology at Columbia University, who gave Maslow her notes from a series of lectures she delivered at Bryn Mawr College in 1941. After her death Dr. Maslow discovered that the notes she had given him were the only ones in existence. She had not published her ideas, and Margaret Mead, her executrix, hunted through all the files and papers, but could not find the manucript of these lectures.

Ruth Benedict was highly dissatisfied with the concept of cultural relativity, which was popular among anthropologists of her day, and with which her name had been closely associated. She struggled to develop a way of comparing various societies as a unitary whole, or, in 20th-Century terms, as a system.

She took four pairs of cultures, which she had selected because they were different, and, on huge sheets of newsprint, wrote all that she knew about these cultures. Four of the cultures had people who were surly and nasty. The other four cultures had produced nice people. At first she talked about low-morale and high-morale cultures. She spoke of hatred and aggression in some groups, as opposed to affection in the others. She tried to identify what there was about some groups that she disliked, and what she liked in the others. She tried relabeling them as secure and insecure cultures. The four good cultures—those she liked—were the Zuni, the Arapesh, the Dakota, and an Eskimo society. The nasty, surly ones were the Chuckchee, the Ojibwa, the Dobwo, and the Kwakiutl. She tried all kinds of generalizations about these cultures. She compared them on the basis of race, geography, climate, size, wealth, and complexity, but none of these criteria seemed to explain the differences.

She finally decided that the basic differences were in what she called the function of behavior, rather than the actual behavior itself. In other words, it was not *how* they behaved so much as *why* they behaved that way. For example, suicide means entirely different things in different cultures. In America, it is generally an admission of the inability to cope with life. In Japan, suicide was the honorable act of a warrior who had made a mistake; it was an act of honor, not despair. In some primitive societies suicide was the final act of a loving wife or sister in the mourning ceremony. There were times in Chinese history when suicide "on the doorstep" (as they said) of another person, was a method of revenging oneself on that person.

The terms that Ruth Benedict finally chose to describe the two types of society were "high synergy" and "low synergy." The high synergy societies were those where people cooperated together for mutual advantage, not necessarily because they were unselfish, but because the customs of society made cooperation worthwhile. In her words, "Societies where non-aggression is conspicuous, have social orders in which the individual, by the same act and at the same time, serves his own advantage and that of the group. . . . Non-aggression occurs, not because people are unselfish and put social obligations above personal desires, but when social arrangements make these two identical. . . . Their institutions insure mutual advantage from their undertakings." [1] (Or, as Dr. Maslow phrased it, "The society with high synergy is one in which virtue pays." [1])

Professor Benedict described the bad societies as: "Societies with low social synergy where the advantage of one individual becomes a victory over another, and the majority who are not victorious must shift as they can." [1]

Dr. Maslow describes these two types of societies, based on notes which he took while discussing the subject with Ruth Benedict. She told Maslow that there seemed to be a difference in the way wealth was distributed in the high and low synergic societies. Regardless of the amount of riches in the good society, wealth seemed to have been spread around more. In the bad society wealth made more wealth and poverty more poverty. Examples of this were the exorbitant rents, the usurious interest with the Kwakiutl (the rate of interest was 1200 percent a year), slave labor, forced labor, exploitation of labor, excessive profits, relatively greater taxation of the poor than the rich, and so on.

Maslow remarked that the god, or gods, in the secure society tended to be rather benevolent, helpful, and friendly, while in the insecure society the gods and other supernatural beings were uniformly ruthless and terrifying.

Maslow tested this relationship with some students at Brooklyn College around 1940. He divided several dozen students into secure and insecure categories and asked those who were religious the following questions: "Suppose you woke up out of your sleep and found somehow that God was either in the room or looking in on you, how would you feel?" [1] The tendency revealed was that the secure student felt comforted and protected while the insecure felt terrified.

Maslow goes on to remark that Western world religious documents show a mixture of what might be called secure and insecure religion. He reports that in the insecure societies the person who has religious power generally uses this for personal profit of some sort. Whereas religious power in a secure society is intended to be used, as by the Zunis, for instance, for bringing rain, for making crops better, for benefiting the whole society. These contrasting approaches—synergic or non-synergic—can be distinguished in the style of prayer, the style of leadership, the style of family relationships, the style of relationships between men and women, the vocabulary of sexuality, the type of friendships and so forth. Societies with high synergy all seem to have techniques for working off humiliation, while societies with low synergy do not. In Benedict's four insecure societies, humiliation rankled and never ended.

Dr. Maslow describes the American society as one of mixed synergy. In many respects our society is a generous, secure one. On the other hand there are customs and institutions which set us against each other. He cites the simple example of the grading system used in most colleges, which makes one man's gain another man's loss. Ruth Benedict's ideas offer the basis for a scientific description of a good or bad society.

This fits perfectly into Dr. Maslow's conception of a scientific basis in human nature for right and wrong behavior. The definition of good and bad societies is merely an extension of this concept. The synergy concept can also be applied to individual behavior. When two individuals arrange their relationship in such a way that one person's advantage is the other person's advantage also, the arrangement is synergic; when one person's advantage is another person's disadvantage, the arrangement is anti-synergic. Maslow cites some recent studies of sex life and family life in lower economic classes in the United States and England. These studies described exploitatious sex relationships—relationships with low synergy. They revealed that the lower class people studied were unable to see a mutually advantageous arrangement between two people. To them love and/or a sex relationship meant advantage to one and a disadvantage to the other, "with the conclusion that whoever loves more is a sucker or must get hurt." [1]

Ruth Benedict's ideas left a deep and lasting impression on Dr. Maslow, and he has continued to seek definitions of the synergic society. He feels that a society can be synergic with human nature, or it can be antagonistic to it. The ideal society is one where virtue pays, and a person pursuing his own interest benefits his society, too.

For such a society to work, it is necessary for the citizens to have the ability to choose efficient leaders, the ability to detect actual superiority. This needs to be coupled with a minimum of jealousy and antagonism toward these superior leaders. The synergic society, or what Maslow in his later works referred to as the Eupsychian society, is a society which creates an environment where people can develop their potential and satisfy their innate psychological needs. The good society is one which is fulfilling and makes self-actualization possible. "A healthy society would be one which fulfills the most potentialities of the greatest number of men." [2] Maslow flatly rejects the idea that the interests of the individual and his society are necessarily mutually exclusive and antagonistic. This is a basic premise of Freudian theory. Maslow envisions a society with psychologically healthy people where there will be less crime, less mental illness, less need for restrictive legislation. Such a society, rather than protecting itself from people's instincts, as Freud saw it, would encourage the strengthening of instincts and would encourage people to develop their potential for love, cooperation, achievement, and growth.

PART TWO

"*Thoughts are but dreams till their effects be tried.*"

SHAKESPEARE

CHAPTER 14

Mental Health

In the preceding chapters we have described Dr. Maslow's theory of human motivation and behavior and have contrasted his point of view with the ideas which have dominated psychology, psychiatry, and the social sciences for the past four or five decades. If Third Force theory is correct, it indicates some revolutionary changes in the current ideas of mankind. It demands a reexamination of presently popular ideas regarding child training, education, psychiatry, law, criminology, business management, economics, and politics. In Dr. Maslow's own words, "This is not an *improvement* of something; it is a real change in direction altogether. It is as if we have been going north and are now going south instead." [1]

In the pages to follow we shall describe the ideas and work of psychologists, psychiatrists, behavioral scientists, managers, consultants, and others whose findings relate to Dr. Maslow's theory. A few of these examples have resulted directly from the work of Maslow, but many represent the work of men who have reached similar conclusions independently. The examples presented are only part of the available evidence. Many other excellent case histories have been omitted. The material available was sufficient for a book in itself, and new information is coming almost daily. Some of the material covered here might be classified as protoknowledge. When each case is considered independently the results may not seem conclusive, but when examined collectively there is an impressive body of factual evidence which supports *the thesis of this book. A breakthrough of world-wide significance has occurred in our understanding of man and his behavior.*

Not all of the people cited on the following pages agree totally with Maslow, nor he with them. However, the reader will discern common threads: a dissatisfaction with pathology-centered theories; recognition of man's potential to grow and to determine his own future; a cognizance that man does not live by bread alone, but has common higher needs; an approach that considers man's feelings, desires, and emotions instead of examining him as one would a lump of coal; a recognition that there is such a thing as right and wrong which can be determined through observation and experience; the belief that responsibility is healthy and irresponsibility is costly.

What seems to be happening all across the United States is that men are discovering that regardless of what the behavior problem is—crime, delinquency, mental illness, alcoholism, drug addiction, or failure (individual or organizational)—the problem is basically ignorance, irresponsibility, a faulty perception of reality. The solution lies in a better understanding of self, others, and sound human relations.

Mental Health

Early critics of the orthodox approaches to the treatment of mental problems include such prominent psychologists and psychiatrists as Carl Jung, Alfred Adler, Gordon Allport, and Carl Rogers. These men can be properly described as early Third Force. Although they have had considerable influence on professional theory their individual efforts have not been sufficient to dislodge the psychoanalytical-Behavioristic domination in American universities and among professional therapists.

Carl Jung read Freud's *Interpretation of Dreams* soon after its publication, and the two men established a close personal relationship. Freud believed that Jung would be his successor, and through Freud's influence he became the first president of the Psychoanalytical Association founded in 1910. Soon, however, Jung's enthusiasm for psychoanalysis began to wane, and in 1915 the two men parted company with no further communication between them.

Jung developed his own theory of human motivation, which emphasized the influence of what he called the collective unconscious and the personal unconscious. He was critical of Freud's overemphasis on subconscious drives without recognition of the important influence of the individual's aims and aspirations. He was also critical of Freud's emphasis on man's lower animal nature alone. He recognized a natural human tendency toward higher values. He believed there was a strong need, and that it was instinctual, for spiritual satisfaction. He advocated a more positive approach, saying, "I prefer to understand man in the perspective of his health." [2] He, too, believed in self-actualization and defined it as the harmonious, balanced, mature personality. Jung's analytical theory still has many advocates, but it is criticized by the majority of behavioral scientists for its treatment of religion, which orthodoxy considers to be "unscientific."

Alfred Adler was born in Vienna in 1870, fourteen years after the birth of Sigmund Freud. Many texts refer to Adler as a disciple of Freud. This erroneous classification was deeply disturbing to Adler, and he denied it many times. Dr. Maslow tells of an incident late in Adler's life when Maslow asked Adler a question that implied he was a disciple under Freud. Adler became very angry and said that this was a lie and a swindle, which he blamed on Freud, and that he had never been a disciple or follower.

Dr. Adler called his theory individual psychology. He, too, was highly critical of Freud's emphasis on the negative or animalistic characteristics of man. He identified Freudian man as neurotic and unhealthy and, like Maslow, believed that healthy man develops goals that are primarily social. He believed the primary motivation was a striving for superiority which was innate in the human species, causing what he called the "great upward drive."

Although man's nature calls for cooperation and sociability, this psychological predisposition will not result from permissive education but must be developed by guidance and training. He placed far less emphasis on unconscious drives, which he considered more characteristic of the neurotic. Healthy individuals are more conscious of the reasons for their behavior and have the ability to choose the direction of their own development. As early as 1914 Adler concluded that all forms of maladjustment were, in fact, attempts to avoid responsibility. "It is a categorical demand of the patient's life plan," he wrote, "that he should fail through the guilt of others and thus be free from responsibility." He called this the "life lie of the neurotic." Thus, man's quest for mental health is related to his education for responsibility.

Gordon Allport, Ph.D., the late distinguished professor of psychology at Harvard, can hardly be described as orthodox. Through most of his academic career he was the devil's advocate to his profession. He was outspokenly pro-religion in a secular and frequently anti-religious academic community. At a time of increasing specialization, he pleaded for behavioral generalists. He found it hard to agree with the overly scientific type of psychology that labeled humans as organisms rather than people. Dr. Allport referred to his profession as "badly dismembered in contradictory theories,"[3] and was refreshingly frank in acknowledging how few practical solutions were known to the profession. He tells the story about a high State Department official who asked whether psychologists had anything that would help him in his day to day work. Allport replied, "Honestly, I do not know, but I am furious with you for not using it."[3] At another time he said, "How in the helping professions—and here I include psychiatry, the ministry, social work, applied psychology, and education—can we recover some of the common sense that we seem to have lost along the way?"[3] In his typically modest manner he praised Freud for increasing the tendency toward self scrutiny, but rejected his emphasis on a lowly opinion of man. "Conscience, we discover, has a wider horizon than he (Freud) knew. Religion also. According to Freud the religious sentiment is an elaboration of our childhood view of the earthly Father. . . . But a more full-bodied study of the role of the religious sentiment in normal adults will surely show how slender is Freud's reductionist formula . . ."[3] Allport also said, "It is an odd fact that psychologists by preference conduct scores of investigations on aggression for every one on affiliation and love. They study stress but not relaxation; pain but not joy; deprivation but not fulfillment; prejudice but not friendship. Just why the seamier aspects of life have chiefly attracted psychologists up to now I don't know." [3] Of behaviorism he said, "Deterministic theories tend to so restrict our science as to render it incapable of having fruitful bearing upon practical life. . . . The trouble with our current theories of learning is not so much that they are wrong, but that they are partial. They fit best the learning of animals and young children. When a convinced positivist tends to fit his image of man to concrete human situations as B. F. Skinner has done in *Walden II*, the result strikes many of us as threadbare, even pitiable." [3] Allport, like Maslow, believed that psychology and psychiatry could not be value free. He told of Philippe Pinel who evolved a revolutionary approach to mental illness 150 years ago. "It was a program of planned rehabilitation in a positive, sympathetic, social milieu marked by friendly association, discussion of difficulties, a busy day of occupational work in family-like environment, during all of which activities the patient was to be treated as a normal person so that he might retain or regain his self respect." [3] It was Dr. Allport's opinion that this essentially "moral treatment" was probably more successful than the more recent so-called "scientific methods."

The Person In Psychology, completed just before Dr. Allport's death in 1967 and published in 1968, refers to a "significant revolution that is occurring." He refers to it as a more sophisticated type of moral treatment or "attitudinal therapy." He sees it as a gradual rediscovery of the pioneering work of Philippe Pinel and others—a healthy movement way from Freudian, Behavioristic orthodoxy. Among the theories moving in this more desirable direction he identifies the work of such men as Adler, Jung, Hartman, Horney, Erikson, Fromm, Goldstein, Rogers, and Maslow. "Only now," he writes, "at long last are the laws of mental illness and health being discovered, and even today, relatively few people know that such laws exist." [3]

Another early critic of "scientific" psychology is *Carl Rogers*, Ph.D., former professor of psychology, director of the psychotherapy research section of the Wisconsin Psychiatric Institute, and presently a resident fellow at Western Behavioral Sciences Institute in La Jolla, California. "I know," said Rogers in 1961, "that I speak for only a fraction of psychologists. The majority—their interests suggested by such terms as stimulus response, learning theory, operant conditioning—are so committed to seeing the individual solely as an object, that what I have to say often baffles if it does not annoy them. I also know that I speak to but a fraction of psychiatrists. For many, perhaps most of them, the truth about psychotherapy has already been voiced long ago by Freud, and they are uninterested in new possibilities, and uninterested in or antagonistic to research in this field. I also know that I speak to but a portion of the divergent groups which call themselves counselors. The bulk of this group are primarily interested in predictive tests and measurements, and in methods of guidance." [4]

Dr. Rogers has never quite reached full agreement with Dr. Maslow's radical concept of species-wide and apparently unchanging common needs, but he comes extremely close to it. His non-directive therapy is designed to help people find their true self, which he describes as "beautiful and constructively realistic," and also as "positive, constructive, moving toward self-actualization, growing toward maturity, growing toward socialization." [4] All people have "basically the same needs, including the need for acceptance from others." [5] He refers to the most revolutionary idea coming from his vast clinical experience as "the growing recognition that the innermost core of man's nature, the deepest layers of his personality, the base of his animal nature is positive in nature—is basically socialized, forward-moving, rational, and realistic." [4]

Roberto Assagioli was born in Venice, Italy, in 1888 and received his medical degree from the University of Florence in Neurology and Psychiatry. Early in his career, Dr. Assagioli became disenchanted with what he considered psychiatry's overemphasis on pathology. In 1926 he opened the Institute of Psychosynthesis which was designed to practice a more positive type of therapy. Twelve years later the Institute was closed due to the antagonism of the Italian Fascist Government. Dr. Assagioli was liberated by the Allied troops in 1944 and reopened the Institute in Florence.

The Institute of Psychosynthesis has gained international recognition. In 1957 the Psychosynthesis Research Foundation was established in the United States, and similar centers of psychosynthesis are now active in France, Greece, Argentina, and England. In his recent book, *Psychosynthesis,* Dr. Assagioli refers to the similarity of his ideas and those of Abraham Maslow and other Third Force psychologists. Frank Hilton, President of the Psychosynthesis Research Foundation states, "As for our own work in this general field of Third Force, there has been a steady, gradual, and encouraging growth of interest in Psychosynthesis over the past seven or eight years. However, we have to be factual and recognize that, as yet, there is but a small percentage of the psychologists and psychiatrsts in North America—or elsewhere for that matter—who think this way, or are even open to the ideas." [6]

Dr. Assagioli sees healthy man as being personally integrated, in harmony with his inner or true self, and moving toward self-realization and sound relationships with others. Organic unity is a goal which many strive for, but few achieve. "In the same way that the normal biological organism experiences an insuppressible tendency toward growth, there is a growth tendency in the human being which lasts throughout life or, at least, much longer than the period of biological growth. When this growth remains unrecognized, or is repressed, or frustrated by environmental obstacles, psychosomatic disturbances are produced." [7]

"Another specific contribution made by Psychosynthesis," Dr. Assagioli writes, "is its reaffirmation of the importance and value of the *will,* drawing attention to its special position as being different from that of other psychic functions. One might say that the will is the Cinderella of modern psychology. Since William James it has been almost entirely neglected, not only by academic psychologists, but also by the leading exponents of dynamic psychology. . . . The man of weak will is like a cork on the ocean tossed by every wave . . . he is a slave, not only of the will of others, and all external circumstances, but also of his drives and desires." [7]

Dr. Assagioli believes that a variety of techniques may be used to develop the integrated personality. He does not object to psychoanalysis as a technique, but does object to Freud's failure to recognize man's higher nature and his therapeutic overemphasis on the past rather than the present and the future. The following story is from the files of *Dr. Jack Cooper,* a New York psychiatrist who practices Psychosynthesis.

"Fran" was a very difficult patient. She had been treated by some of the best psychoanalysts in the country, but they were unable to help her. When she came to Psychosynthesis she was in bad shape and had been hospitalized for over five years with what was termed everything from chronic undifferentiated schizophrenia to psycho-neurotic anxiety. She had been taking all kinds of of pills, had received intravenous nembutal shots and repeated shock treatments, and for eight months had a psychiatric nurse in constant attendance. When she was transferred to the locked ward in a New York State hospital, three additional nurses had to be called to help the one who, bleeding from the mouth, was attempting to lead her into the ward. When they put her in the tubs to relax her, she would scream for three or four hours in terror. Her legs were all cut up, and her hands and wrists were swollen with scar tissue.

She says that when she first saw Dr. Cooper, she thought "Oh Lord, here comes another idiot psychiatrist—the ninth; so we will see what he has to say." [8] Fran's problem was not lack of will—it would be better described as uncontrollable or misdirected will. She went through life attempting to impose her will on everyone, including the doctors and psychiatrists, and destroying her life in the process. Dr. Cooper utilized techniques of Psychosynthesis to direct her powerful will toward useful purposes. She describes this as follows:

"What Dr. Cooper did mostly in the beginning was to have me practice this 'willing' as opposed to resolution, being willing. This is hard to put into words; it is being willing to start from where you are; willing to have no particular goal in mind; willingness to be in the moment. I would start out and go maybe one or two doors from the hospital and look in a store window. Dr. Cooper told me to do this and to memorize the objects on display and then turn away and see if I could remember them. Also little exercises like following an instrument in a band or in a recording, trying to follow the clarinet through. Or try to concentrate on one thing; and be willing to accept that by the standard of society I am a failure and a very limited person; but yet in a sense I am not limited—at least I believe so. I am willing to see things as they are and I am trying to live one day at a time and I am not trying to prove anything any more. . . ." [8]

Dr. Cooper taught her to do things daily which she didn't have to do. For example, she would take a box of matches and dump out the matches and then put them back in the box one at a time. She began to have a feeling of accomplishment, a feeling of progress, or as Dr. Cooper says, "In Fran's instance, the breakthrough came after she was to feel the strength of making a decision and following through—putting the matches back in a box or some simple procedure." [8]

At the end of 2½ years, Fran was not without problems, but she had made tremendous progress. She was able to attend Alcoholics Anonymous meetings and admit that she was an alcoholic. She went to charm school.

She began looking for a job. Fran was not discouraged from talking about the past, but the emphasis was on the present and the future. "She would start detailing all that had happened in the past," said Dr. Cooper, "and I would say, 'that is very interesting, but what are your problems today?' " [8]

Fran herself summed up, "I am accepting the fact that I am this way and I can function with these limitations, and I have hope . . ." [8]

Dr. Abraham M. Low, M.D. was a professor of psychiatry at the University of Illinois Medical School. Low founded Recovery, Inc., an organization for people with mental problems, in Chicago in 1937. Today there are over 400 chapters across the country. Recovery, Inc., might be compared to Alcoholics Anonymous. It is a self-help program for people with emotional problems, many of them former inmates of mental hospitals. The members discover that their problems are not unique, that others have similar experiences of fear, inadequacy, hopelessness, and delusion. The methods developed by Dr. Low frequently obtain remarkable results.

Low cited the following comparative figures: The Psychoanalytic Institutes of Berlin, London, Chicago, and the Menninger Clinic in Kansas were able to treat 660 cases (eliminating those who did not continue therapy for six months or more) in a period of ten years (five years in Chicago). Low, by his group methods, was able to treat 156 mental patients in a representative two-year period. Thus, according to his statistics, his method enabled one psychiatrist to treat 780 patients in ten years, as compared to the 660 treated by four well-staffed and richly financed psychoanalytical institutions.

Mental Health Through Will-Training (1950) is a detailed account of Dr. Low's method of therapy. The book presents statistics regarding the ineffectiveness of Freudian psychoanalysis, which, in Dr. Low's opinion, dominated psychiatric treatment and had all but eliminated its closest rivals (Adler and Jung). At that time, he reported that the Menninger Clinic was achieving approximately a 40% recovery with psychotic cases. This compared with statistics from mental hospitals showing a spontaneous recovery rate of 40%. Low's conclusion was that psychoanalysis was a failure. (More recent studies by Eysenck show a higher rate of success for psychoanalysis, but also a higher rate for spontaneous recovery.)

Dr. Low says of himself, "The author rejects the psychoanalytical doctrine both as philosophy and therapeutic technique. In point of philosophy, he cannot share the view that human conduct is the result of unconscious drives, sexual or otherwise. To his way of thinking, adult life is not *driven* by instincts but guided by will." [9] Mental problems, to be solved, require a positive approach and recognition of man's ability to choose and control his own destiny—an approach almost the exact opposite of Freud's. Low stated, "By labeling sensations as 'intolerable,' feelings as 'terrible,' impulses as 'uncontrollable,' the lingo discourages the patient from facing, tolerating, and controlling the reaction." [9]

The doctor was not enthusiastic about dream therapy or attempts to trace psychotic problems to infantile, instinctual, or sexual drives of the patient. He placed the emphasis on the present and the future, and was an early advocate of group therapy with a minimum of professional participation. He demonstrated that patients could overcome their neurotic fears and phobias by confronting the very things they feared. The major responsibility rested with the patient, not the doctor. "You were not responsible for getting sick," he said, "but it is now your responsibility for getting well. There is no such thing as 'I can't.' When you say 'I can't' you are declaring yourself exceptional. So long as no vital organs are damaged, you can do anything any other average person can do." [10]

Dr. Low did not make himself popular with other psychiatrists by his outspoken criticism of Freudian theory. Now, however, his ideas are gradually gaining greater acceptance. In May, 1968, for the first time, a spokesman for Recovery, Inc., was invited to participate in a panel discussion at the annual convention of the American Psychiatric Association. "Psychiatrists are beginning to feel that Recovery, Inc., is a valuable adjunct," commented Dr. Alex Spadoni of Stritch School of Medicine and Director of Psychiatry at St. Joseph Hospital, Joliet, Illinois. "It should be incorporated into existing mental-health services. It is particularly helpful for chronic patients." [10]

Henry C. Link, Ph.D., was was another early critic of value-free psychology. His now famous book, *The Return to Religion* (1936), was for many years the subject of wide discussion and controversy. A highly successful clinical psychologist, Link was thoroughly grounded in "scientific psychology." His professional training had convinced him of the absurdity of the religious conviction of his parents. During the depression years of the early 30's Link was special advisor to the Adjustments Service of New

York City, which gave psychological examinations to 15,321 unemployed men and women. Dr. Link was personally responsible for the planning and supervision of a statistical study of 10,000 of these unemployed people. Under his direction, they were given a total of 73,226 psychological tests, accompanied by a detailed personal history of each individual. Analysis of this data enabled Dr. Link to discover aspects of human behavior which had not been obvious from his years of clinical experience. He found that in most cases personality problems were the major factor in people's unemployment. One of the findings which startled Link was that, contrary to what he had been taught, those individuals who were most active in churches had better personalities than those who were not. By better personalities he meant better adjustment to life and better qualifications for employment. He found himself advising his clients to become more active socially, to develop social skills, to become less self-centered. Church attendance, he found, was an excellent prescription. It became increasingly obvious to Dr. Link that the major problems of his clients were lack of values, lack of beliefs, and lack of life objectives.

He found that the typical problem person was an introvert—that is, very self-centered, avoiding people, avoiding risks, unable to make friends. Extroverts, on the other hand, were better adjusted, more considerate of others, happier, and more successful. These characteristics did not seem to have a genetic basis but were acquired, frequently in childhood. Link found it was possible, although difficult, to change the attitudes of adult introverts and help them develop social skills. He found the Bible helpful, too, in teaching people the social skills that made them happier and more successful. Christ, he said, was an extrovert and taught others to be extroverts. Dr. Link became highly critical of "value-free" psychology and psychiatry. "The predominant scientific and social philosophy of our age," he wrote, "is that man as an individual is helpless, a creature without self-respect, without will power, without faith in himself.

"This definition of man, psychologists are finding, is not only horribly degrading, but fundamentally untrue." [11] He pleaded for better balance in public education, with less emphasis on scientific knowledge and more emphasis on the basic values which make knowledge worthwhile. He called agnosticism an intellectual disease. He deplored the trend toward "over education"—a problem common to his clinical patients. He found that frequently these people's problems stemmed from too much theory and too little practice. They were what he called "educated fools." He cited the growing body of evidence that no significant growth in personality resulted from higher education. "Indeed," he said, "there is some good evidence that the contrary often occurs, and that the prolongation of formal education results in a deterioration of personality." [12]

O. Hobart Mowrer, Ph.D., is another distinguished psychologist who broke with theories of behavior that picture man as a helpless victim of heredity or environment. Now Research Professor of Psychology at the University of Illinois, Hobart Mowrer has had a distinguished career. He received his doctorate in psychology from Johns Hopkins University and has taught at Yale and Harvard. He is a past president of the American Psychological Association. In the early 30's he was a member of the group who studied at the Institute of Human Relations, Yale University, with Clark Hull, a leading advocate of behavioristic theory. The Institute of Human Relations sought to develop a multi-disciplinary approach to human problems combining psychology, psychiatry, sociology, and anthroplogy.

In addition to his thorough understanding of Behaviorist theory, Mowrer had a firsthand knowledge of Freudian psychoanalysis. He had spent 15 years in and out of psychoanalysis in an attempt to solve his own personal problems. Dr. Mowrer has written and lectured extensively on the failure of both psychiatry and religion to deal effectively with mental and emotional disturbances. His book, *The Crisis in Psychiatry and Religion,* was published in 1961.

He has developed an effective new method known as Integrity Therapy for treating emotional problems, which is especially popular among psychologists and psychiatrists with religious convictions. His philosophy is almost the opposite of Freudian theory. Mowrer finds that instead of mental problems resulting from the individual's attempts to live up to unnaturally high moral codes, they occur when man does not live up to his own moral convictions. He states, "We have found good reason to believe that psychopathology instead of stemming from unexpressed sex and hostility, comes rather from an outraged conscience and violated sense of human decency and responsibility. This radically revised perception of the basis and nature of mental illness suggests an affinity with both classical and contemporary conceptions of the holy spirit and points the way to a new synthesis of religion and contemporary psychological and social science." He continues, "The problem presented by psychopathology . . . is one that is best conceptualized, not as illness, but rather as a kind of ignorance and moral failure. And the strategy of choice in preventing and correcting these conditions is manifestly educational and ethical." [13]

At another time, Dr. Mowrer said of psychoanalysis, "Freud's theory was also seductively attractive to the neurotic individual himself—it absolved him of any accountability for his condition and offered him a form of therapy which promised to relieve and release simultaneously . . . now we have research findings which explicitly repudiate the premise on which the whole psychoanalytic approach is founded.[14] Numerous studies (Eysenck, 1952; Eysenck, 1961; Knight, 1941; Wilder, 1945) have shown that psychoanalytical therapy, despite the great amount of time and expense involved, is not demonstratively effective; and its impact upon various social institutions—home, church, school, and courts—seems often to have been, not helpful, but disintegrative." [15]

Willard H. Mainord, Ph.D., University of Louisville psychologist, agrees with Third Force theory in many important respects. First, he is dissatisfied with orthodox therapy, especially psychoanalysis. Second, he believes that the mentally disturbed are not sick in the medical sense, but are irresponsible. Third, he believes the therapist must help the patient to discover that irresponsibility does not pay and responsibility does. Fourth, he thinks that a good society is one where virtue is rewarded.

"If the patient," says Dr. Mainord, "is held responsible for productivity and for accurate communication, the 'crazy' behavior will have no payoff value and will disappear—sometimes dramatically." [16] He gives the following examples from his experiences at Western State Hospital to illustrate this point.

"One of our patients insisted he had never been born and would then (naturally) never die, and further, had the power to destroy others upon whim or upon request. This type of thing was accepted rather blandly by the staff for some years, but he gradually became something of a management problem. When it was decided that he should be locked up, one of the authors was given the task of getting the job done. The patient refused to talk and threatened to destroy us if we insisted. We insisted and had a burly nursing assistant escort the patient to our office. The patient threatened us again with immediate destruction if we did not quit bothering him. The patient was told that he had better get on with the job then, as he was going to be bothered until he collected his things and moved to a locked ward. This promise was made with sincerity and conviction. In about a half minute, the patient said he did not want any trouble with us and would do as we asked. We never again heard of the power of immediate destruction. One might guess that the patient knew he was expressing nonsense, but as long as he could exploit it, he was quite willing to continue." [17]

"Another patient insisted he was unable to do any work because his back had been broken and stuffed with manure. When it was finally decided that broken backs were reason enough to refuse weekend passes, a rather remarkable orthopedic recovery ensued. The exploitive aspects of such delusions are obvious. We are arguing that it is the exploitation that needs to be noted—not the paranoid thinking." [17]

Dr. Mainord developed his system at Western State Hospital in the state of Washington. His patients were a typical mental hospital cross-section, usually classified by psychiatrists as about 50% schizophrenic and about 50% depressive, and included alcoholics and drug addicts. Regardless of the diagnosis, Mainord treated all of his patients the same. Their problem was ignorance, irresponsibility, a poor perception of reality, a lack of self-understanding, and an inability to behave in a socially acceptable manner. His diagnosis of mental illness is simple and almost brutal, but it works. "You're not sick," he says, "you're crazy." [16]

Here, in his own words, are some of his major ideas: "Teaching the patient to believe that he is sick is to encourage him to become a passive recipient of whatever treatment the physician recommends. If the patient chooses to wait till he is 'cured,' chronic hospital residence might be predicted. . . .[18] In the traditional mental hospital, . . . it is not at all unusual in such settings to see completely unacceptable behavior followed by pleasant consequences, and vice versa.[16]

The new patient . . . will usually explain his presence, not in terms of his own inadequacy, but in terms of a misunderstanding or an actually hostile social environment." [16]

Mainord said in a speech at the Western Psychological Association annual meeting in 1962: "It has been some years now since Eysenck began publishing evidence that psychotherapeutic procedures customarily employed have been ineffective. The usual response has been that there is something wrong with Eysenck, inasmuch as everyone *knows* that psychotherapy works. If any proof is needed, ask therapists and some of their patients, and it is obvious that therapy works miracles in a strangely leisurely way. And if therapies have occasionally not worked, it has been a matter of unskilled therapists, unmotivated patients, and the untreatability of many diagnostic groups. With these cozy explanations always available, we have continued merrily to train more therapists to carry out the same fruitful procedures, and have taught them, in the process, that it is only the naive and/or foolish who actually expect to modify patient behavior with any marked degree of success in less than years and years of excavating, catharting, transferring, insight seeking, and Freud knows what else." [18]

Mainord created an artificial society within the mental hospital. Members join the group voluntarily and are refused admittance only when they are unable to verbalize. They soon learn that all important decisions will be made by the group (medical decisions excepted). Such privileges as passes, jobs, visits, and even discharge will be group decisions. The patient must agree to take full responsibility for his own actions and, also, responsibility for the actions of others in the group. They are committed to be completely honest with the group, and no exceptions are permitted. The method is confrontation, and Mainord has discovered that strong words are more effective than weak ones. He gives the example of a female patient who had spent many years in various psychotherapies without much success, and continued a pattern of destructive drinking bouts. After she had described her problem to the therapy group, the group identified her behavior as lying, blackmail, evasion of responsibility, and being a parasite. The patient summed up the group's conclusion by saying, "You're telling me I'm not sick. You're telling me I'm a slob." [16] This proved to be a turning point for this individual because, whatever else she might be, she was determined not to be a slob. The group demands responsible behavior and is structured in a manner to prove to the patient that responsibility and productivity, when combined with developing skills, will result in "warm, affectionate, genuinely valuable human relationships." [16]

Patients must demonstrate and develop their responsibility by doing useful work in the mental institution. The standards of performance are strict. The group members must perform whatever task they are assigned with the same competence that would be expected of a paid member of the hospital staff. Substandard performance would keep the patient at a low level of reward. Good performance, on the other hand, entitles the patient to request a more challenging occupational task and greater freedom. The gradual development of individual responsibility over a period of months results in greater and greater freedom, and also greater respect and confidence, leading ultimately to complete discharge from the hospital. "My patients have taught me," says Dr. Mainord, "to believe that no one ever goes crazy because he has insisted upon doing the right thing." [16]

Dr. Mainord reports the following typical results. One hundred thirty women, classified as about 50% schizophrenic and 50% depressive, were treated over a period of one year. The average stay in the group was slightly over two months, and, as the group met every day for about an hour and a half, the average graduate received 60 or 70 hours of therapy. Of the 130 who entered the program, five dropped out of treatment for one reason or another, 100 had been discharged from the hospital, and 25 were still in treatment. One year later, of the 100 discharged 12 had returned for further treatment, but 10 of these were quickly redischarged.

Another psychiatrist who has turned his back on orthodox theories is *Dr. William Glasser*. In his book, *Reality Therapy* (1965), Glasser wrote, "Toward the end of my psychiatric training I found myself in the uncomfortable position of doubting much that I had been taught." [19] Glasser set out to develop a new approach. His answers bear a remarkable resemblance to those of Maslow. People who need psychiatric treatment have not been able to satisfy their basic human needs for relatedness and respect. To satisfy these needs, they must learn to be realistic, learn the difference between right and wrong behavior. "Irresponsible people," he writes, "always seeking to gain happiness without assuming responsibility, find only brief periods of joy, but not the deep-seated satisfaction which accompanies responsible behavior." [19]

"The crux of my theory," Dr. Glasser states, "is personal responsibility, which we equate with mental health—the more responsible a person, the healthier he is—the less responsible, the less healthy. . . . The teaching of responsibility is the most important task of higher animals, man most certainly included . . . that it can be taught only to the young is not true." [19] Dr. Glasser defines responsibility as "The ability to fulfill one's needs, and to do so in a way that does not deprive others of the ability to fulfill their needs. . . . A responsible person also does that which gives him a feeling of self-worth and a feeling that he is worthwhile to others. He is motivated to strive and perhaps endure privation to attain self-worth." [19]

Reality therapy differs from conventional therapy in at least six major aspects:

1. Dr. Glasser rejects the orthodox concept of mental illness and the various categories by which it is described—paranoic, schizophrenic, manic, etc. To Dr. Glasser, most forms of mental disturbance are best described as irresponsibility; and, regardless of what the behavior symptoms are, the solution is to show the patient the unreality of his behavior. The therapist helps the patient to discover behavior which will satisfy his basic psychological needs.

2. Conventional theory places great emphasis on examining the patient's past experience. It is believed that once the patient understands the root causes of his behavior he will be able to change. Reality Therapy is not particulary interested in the patient's past behavior. If it had been acceptable, the person would not be in therapy. The entire focus is upon the present and future.

3. Conventional psychiatry has placed great emphasis on the theory of transference which states that the patient can be induced to transfer to his doctor attitudes that he held or still holds toward people in his past. The psychiatrist then attempts to make the patient aware of this transference and, through this insight, enable him to change his behavior. Glasser relates to the person as himself and not as a transference figure.

4. Conventional psychotherapy believes that if the patient is to change he must gain insight into his unconscious mind. Unconscious conflict is considered more important than conscious problems. Thus, the conventional emphasis is on dreams, transference, and free association. Dr. Glasser does not permit patients to use unconscious motivations as an excuse for their behavior. The emphasis is upon what the patient is doing and intends to do.

5. Because orthodox psychiatry believes in mental illness, it avoids value judgments. "Conventional psychiatry," says Glasser, "scrupulously avoids the problem of morality, that is, whether the patient's behavior is right or wrong. Deviant behavior is considered the product of the mental illness, and the patient should not be held morally responsible because he

is considered helpless to do anything about it." [19] The basic premise of Reality Therapy is almost the exact opposite. The patient's problem is the result of his inability to comprehend and apply moral principles in his daily life.

6. Conventional therapy does not generally include teaching people to behave in a better manner. It is assumed that once patients understand themselves and the unconscious sources of their problems, they will be able to learn better behavior themselves. Reality Therapy, on the other hand, seeks to teach patients better ways to behave—ways of behaving which will enable patients to fulfill their basic psychological needs. Reality Therapy was first put to the test in a California Institution for delinquent girls. This program will be described in the next chapter.

One of the men who encouraged Dr. William Glasser was his professor, *G. L. Harrington,* M.D. Dr. Harrington tested Reality Therapy in the treatment of a group of about 200 psychotic patients in a West Los Angeles veteran's hospital. Identified as Building 206, this section of the hospital contained chronic "mentally ill" patients. Their problems were categorized as paranoia, schizophrenia, catatonic schizophrenia, hemophrenic schizophrenia, and chronic undifferentiated schizophrenia, etc. Little change in their condition was expected, and the average discharge rate was about two patients a year. The conventional treatment called for kindness, sympathy, and tolerance for their idiosyncracies; since they were ill they were not expected to take any responsibility.

Dr. Harrington took charge of Building 206 and, with the help of one psychologist and one social worker, introduced a Reality Therapy program to the staff and patients. Staff members were taught that these long-term patients at some time or another in the past had been unable to fill their psychological needs and were, therefore, unable to function in a responsible manner. Because they were not able to fulfill their needs in the real world, sometimes suddenly but usually more gradually, these individuals began to deny reality and move into worlds of their own. The task to be accomplished by the staff working with the inmates was to help convince the patients that their problem was not permanent and, then, help them slowly to learn to act more responsibly. Nurses and aides were taught by Dr. Harrington to seek to get patients involved. This process with deeply disturbed patients, some of them violent or destructive, took anywhere from a few weeks to six months. Eventually the patient began to realize that someone cared about him. He responded by changing his behavior, sometimes for the better, sometimes for the worse. When the patient began to realize he was accepted as a person, it became possible for him to begin to reject his unsocial behavioral symptoms.

Each patient was helped to gradually assume more and more responsibility, first in the hospital and then on the outside. It soon became apparent to the men in Building 206 that something was happening. The average release rate of two a year a year rose to 25 in the first year, 1962. By 1963 the annual rate of release had jumped to 75 patients, with three returning. In the third year it was 80 releases, with seven returning; in the fourth year 111 veterans returned to society, with only seven of them returning for further treatment. Dr. Harrington returned to private practice in 1965.

Lawrence LeShan, Ph.D., former chief of psychology at the Institute of Applied Biology, New York City, believes that significant changes are taking place in professional circles. In an article published in 1962, he wrote, "a revolution in scientific thought is not always immediately obvious, even to those most closely involved in the field. It may proceed and be running its course and be felt by a large number of publications, each concerned with one phase of the transition and contributing a general theory of discontent with older theories and techniques, without a clear or coordinated sense of the nature of the change that may be taking place.

"This general atmosphere may cause a majority of workers in the area of concern to change their ways of thinking and methods of action—often in similar directions—while retaining the feeling that most of their colleagues are proceeding in the older way.

"It is the thesis of this paper that such a revolution, a major change in theory and technique, has been underway in the field of psychoanalytical-oriented psychotherapy for some time now, and that this change has been taking place at all levels." [20]

Dr. LeShan identifies five major assumptions of psychoanlytical theory that are receiving critical reexamination. The first of these is what he terms psychic determinism. The trend he identifies is away from the concept of man as a helpless victim of unconscious drives from within or environment from without. There is a tendency to question Freud's dictum "we do not live, we are lived by unknown and uncontrollable forces." "The theory of determinism," states LeShan, "has led psychotherapy into two difficult positions. The first of these has been the therapist's attempts to excuse the patient's negative and undesirable behavior on the grounds that it was determined by his past, and so he had no reason to feel guilty about it. On the other hand, he attempted to accept positive and desirable behavior as free so that the patient could gain in self-liking and self-respect." [20]

A second major assumption which seems to be changing is the concept of moral relativism. "A basic tenet of psychotherapy has been that moral values have no place in the process. Nothing is morally 'right' or morally 'wrong'. . . . It is now generally realized that this is itself a value system. As Rollo May put it: 'The lack of value judgments which the older therapy opted for is based on a definite philosophical system—that of a fairly complete relativism.' " [20] The recent trend identified by LeShan is toward a recognition of a positive relationship between moral values and mental health. He makes the interesting comment that, at the same time some scientists are rediscovering moral values, some religious leaders are being influenced by the older concept of moral relativism.

The third assumption is regarding the orthodox psychoanalytical idea that the therapist must remain detached from his patient. Dr. William Glasser's Reality Therapy is an excellent example of the newer concept that the psychiatrist must become involved with his client as a human being.

The fourth major assumption which Dr. LeShan believes is changing is the Freudian opposition to dealing with real-life problems in therapy. LeShan gives the following case history as typical of the older point of view: A woman phoned Sarah Connell, chief worker of the Manhattan Society for Mental Health, and asked her advice. "She and her husband had both been in psychoanalysis . . . he for 6 years and she for 4. The husband's analyst was raising his fees; the husband's income had recently declined and he felt too embarrassed to discuss the problem with his analyst. The woman wanted to know if Mrs. Connell thought it would be permissible for her to call her husband's analyst and acquaint him with the facts. Mrs. Connell replied, 'Of course, but you are in therapy. Why don't you discuss this with your analyst?' There was a moment of shocked silence, and then the woman said, 'But Mrs. Connell, this is a *reality* problem.' " [20]

The fifth assumption is that human nature is all bad. "At the present time," writes LeShan, "a reaction appears to be taking place against this viewpoint. A realization is growing that positive drives are just as 'real,' as organic to man's nature and certainly as important as negative ones." [20] To illustrate the former point of view he tells the story of a secretary who went to work for a psychoanalyst but resigned a few weeks later. When asked why she left the job, she explained, "Because I couldn't win. If I came to work late it was because I was hostile, if I came early it was because I was anxious, if I arrived on time I was compulsive." [20]

In a more serious vein, he gives a second example. "In a New York City public school, in 1960, a rather disturbed 8-year-old girl was having a tantrum. She lay on the floor screaming. The principal of the school—an extremely perceptive and sensitive person—picked her up, held her in his arms and cuddled her, recognizing what she needed most at the moment. She started to quiet down and just lay against his shoulder sobbing The school social worker said to the principal (in all seriousness) 'I told you that you would begin to sublimate because you have no daughters. You had better watch your step.' " [20]

The first issue of the *Journal of Humanistic Psychology* was published in 1961 with Anthony Sutich as editor, and the American Association of Humanistic Psychology (AAHP) started the next year. Dr. Maslow's ideas were a major influence in both of these developments. It would be inaccurate, however, to imply that the AAHP was an organization to develop or promote Maslow's philosophy—the Association represents a broad humanistic viewpoint.

Among the founders were prominent advocates of Carl Rogers' nondirective therapy, Gestalt psychology, General Semantics, Adler, and Jung. The new association represented a revolt against mechanistic, deterministic, psychoanalytic, behavioristic orthodoxy.

James F. T. Bugental was the first president and has written extensively about the Humanistic movement. He cautions his readers not to confuse the Humanistic movement with Humanism, as the word has been used traditionally. In its traditional sense, humanism has been used to designate atheism or agnosticism as opposed to theism—the belief in a creator or creative force in the universe. "Humanistic psychology," states Bugental, "includes devout theists and devout atheists and all shadings in between." "Humanistic psychology," he continues, "is not new. William James was certainly a humanistic psychologist. It is the psychology which the layman usually would think of as the 'real' psychology. It is the sort of concern that most closely accords with the literal meaning of 'psychology' (knowledge of the soul), and philosophers from the classic period forward have tended to concern themselves with the kinds of issues that current humanistic psychology studies." [21]

In 1964 Dr. Bugental wrote that "a major breakthrough" was occurring in psychology. He felt that this was the beginning of a new era in man's concern about himself—an era that can "produce as profound changes in the human condition as those we have seen the physical sciences bring about in the past century." [22] He identifies the following characteristics of the broad movement:

1. Man is the central subject matter of psychology. Humanistic psychologists object to the use of data from rats, monkeys, or pigeons as if equal in significance to the study of man himself.

2. Man is more than the total of his parts and must be studied as a unified organism.

3. Humanistic psychology places a high value on individual freedom. It seeks to help the individual to better predict and control his own life. Bugental contrasts this to Behaviorism which has frequently been used to "serve those who would predict and control other people." [21]

4. Humanistic criteria for determining the value of research findings stress the importance of human rather than non-human objectives. There are valid humanistic criteria such as intrinsic meaningfulness, coherence with other conceptions, validation by the observation of independent observers, effectiveness in changing human experience—all of which are every bit as validating as are statistical frequency or laboratory repetitions.

The Humanistic point of view as defined by Dr. Bugental includes such terms as "man is aware," "man has choice," "man is responsible," "Man's potential is greater than he has yet actualized." He contrasts this with the other points of view. "The behaviorist tends to see man as an elaborate assemblage of conditioned responses, interlocking and built into hierarchies, but principally or solely deriving from past experience, triggered by external stimuli and significant only in action terms. . . . The model used by the classical psychoanalyst has some features in common with that of the Behaviorist in that it gives prime emphasis to what is past, treats motivation chiefly in hemostatic terms, makes the interplay of external forces on the organism the main source of how the organism is and what it does. . . . there is relatively little attention to the aware person (as contrasted with the voluminous attention to the unconscious)." [21]

The Association of Humanistic Psychologists has grown steadily and by mid-1969 numbered over 1,200 members. This may be compared with the much older American Psychological Association founded in 1892 with a membership approaching 30,000 and including most of the qualified psychologists in the country. "Humanistic psychology," writes Bugental, "is under the apparent handicap that it is little represented in the major American universities and psychological research centers. By and large, these are in the control of mechanamorphic faculties." [23]

CHAPTER 15

Crime, Delinquency, and Addiction

Criminals, alcoholics, and habitual drug addicts cost our society billions of dollars annually. The statistical evidence regarding crime and drug addiction shows that these problems are increasing much faster than our population. No one knows exactly how many alcoholics there are, but the estimates vary from four to six and one-half million, and the annual cost, including the loss to industry, is placed well over three billion dollars. The annual cost of crime is now estimated to be an incredible 27 billion dollars annually. Despite the serious nature of these problems, money spent in attempts at rehabilitation is surprisingly small. Governmental action is generally punitive or custodial and not often oriented toward rehabilitation. Psychiatrists and clinical psychologists have generally avoided these serious problems.

Limited though it is, the evidence strongly suggests that Third Force psychology provides the long-awaited key to the solution of these costly social problems.

The *Seventh Step Program* to rehabilitate hardened criminals was developed by William Sands, who was himself a former convict.

Bill Sands was not yet 18 when he was sent up for the first time for five holdups with a rusty revolver that wasn't loaded. His reform school experience only hardened his attitudes. He decided to become a professional thief rather than an amateur. He shared a hatred and contempt for authority with other reform school inmates, a hatred which he says is the most common characteristic of all criminals.

Sands didn't come from a poor home. His father was a California Superior Court Judge, but he was an alcoholic. His mother was an attractive society woman, but, in his own words, "she was a sadist." When Bill was nine his mother beat him with a branch torn from a rose bush until his back was raw. The scars remained for many years.

Once out of reform school Bill set out to get even with his father, his mother, the reform school, the guards, and society in general. In July, 1941, he was sentenced to not less than one year nor more than life and sent to San Quentin Prison. He soon became a hardened, hate-filled convict. He tried to kill a fellow con and nearly succeeded. He spent his many weeks in solitary confinement planning his revenge on society.

Considering his record of incorrigibility, his chances for seeing society again seemed slim. But Clinton T. Duffy, the new warden at San Quentin, changed his life. Duffy was a man who believed prisoners could change. A radio commentator once said to Warden Duffy, "You should know that leopards don't change their spots!" Duffy snapped back, "You should know I don't work with leopards. I work with men and men change every day." [1] With Warden Duffy's encouragement, Bill Sands did change and won his parole and became a respectable citizen. In a few years he had a wife, a comfortable home, drove a Mercedes-Benz, and was a popular nightclub entertainer.

But he could not forget his prison experience and decided to devote his energies to helping criminals reform. His Seventh Step program was started at Leavenworth Prison. It was based on the Maslow-related principle that irresponsibility does not pay, and furthermore, criminal behavior cannot satisfy the criminal's needs to relate with other people. Because he was an

ex-convict, Sands was able to break the barrier which exists between convicts and most people in authority—the barrier that makes the average
convict deaf when these people try to reach him. "All cons resent the
treatment they got as children," says Sands, "an unfair teacher, an insin-
cere father, a bitch of a mother, or a myriad of other grievances—so they
commit an act of defiance . . . every sentence they serve they serve in
hatred and resentment. Some are restless to get out, so they can prove
again that they are still rebels against a system that is unfair." [1]

Bill worked with a group of prisoners within the prison. They agreed to
think realistically. Gradually, over a period of time they worked out the
seven steps of the program. The plan depends on convicts changing other
convicts. It is a tough, realistic system which forces these men to recognize
the stupidity of their behavior. The seven steps include such concepts as
"Facing the truth about ourselves in the world around us . . . deciding
we need to change . . . realizing that there is a power from which we can
gain strength . . . honest self-appraisal . . . helping ourselves to overcome our weaknesses . . . setting attainable goals toward which we can
work every day . . . pledging ourselves to help others as we have been
helped . . . deciding that our freedom is worth more than our resentment." [1]

Leavenworth is a maximum-security prison, and the normal rate of prisoners returning to jail after release has been about 80%. Graduates from
the Seventh Step program showed a record of less than 10% return. The
program is now active in several states and has more than 4,000 successful parolees.

The *Mott Vocational Guidance Program* in Flint, Michigan, was organized in 1964 to deal with the problems of hardened criminals. It is an
experimental program to develop methods to change the value-orientation
of these criminals. The organization seeks to prepare convicts to become
contributing members of society rather than more proficient criminals. It
is assumed that no one is born a criminal, and all or, at least, the majority
of criminals have the capacity to change their behavior. Criminal behavior
is neither normal nor healthy.

The guidance program has found that, generally speaking, the best
counselors for this type of work are those who have the ability and talent
to provide meaningful motivation, counseling, and guidance. According to
B. G. Hulsopple, Ph.D. and researcher at Mott, the counselor must pos-

sess these qualities as well: a genuine concern for his fellow man, an ability to empathize or "feel in" with another human being while maintaining personal objectivity, and a meaningful base of knowledge about human behavior. The Mott Vocational Guidance Program has successfully used a proportion of ex-convicts as counselors—this is an important aspect of the Program. Counselors work with the men in prison and, also, after they are out on parole, and prove to these men that they have the capacity to be responsible. It is primarily an educational program, and the prisoners' attitudes are changed through individual counseling, group therapy, and vocational education. A recent report from the Mott Foundation revealed that of a group of 504 criminals who were voluntary participants in the program, only 87, or about 17%, violated their parole after completion of the program. Compare this with the performance of average parolees, whose rate of return under similar circumstances varies from 30% to 70%.

The *Yonan Codex Foundation* was first called to our attention by Professor Leonard J. Hippchen, Department of Criminology and Corrections, Florida State University. Dr. Hippchen had studied the Foundation's activities and written a report on his observations.

The Foundation was started in 1962 by Dan MacDougald, an Atlanta attorney. He had become highly dissatisfied with the way Georgia treated its criminals. "Formerly," MacDougald says, Georgia's prisons operated on the theory that long confinement plus fear of society's vengeance, would solve the problem. Actually this was beneficial to society, for many of the criminals died in jail, leaving society with less criminality. It was very hard on the criminals, however. Today, the approach is to return the criminal mind to the streets as quickly as possible, better trained, better educated, better equipped to successfully obtain his anti-social designs. . . . The thinly veiled contempt which society carries for the convict is acutely sensed by the criminal mind and returned ten-fold in hatred, malice, and viciousness. Society cannot communicate with the convict; the convict cannot communicate with society." [2]

The Yonan Codex Foundation set out to find a better solution. The organization engaged in extensive multidisciplinary research. The program it devised is a remarkable combination of behavioral science, Greek philosophy, and Christian morality. While it draws from religion, it works equally well for Christians, Jews, Mohammedans, agnostics, or atheists. The objective is not religious conversion but emotional maturity. The method is called Emotional Maturity Instruction. Emotional maturity is considered to be natural and healthy for the individual, while emotional immaturity produces neurosis, psychosis, alcoholism, drug addiction, or criminality. Immature adults produce excessive tension in themselves and in others by their unsound behavior. Criminals are out of touch with reality, and the harder they try to reduce their tensions the poorer the results they achieve. "The criminal mentality," writes Mr. MacDougald, "is characterized by a lack of respect for others, for their lives, for their property, or for their loved ones, or for all three.

"The moral rehabilitation of the criminal mentality is accomplished by the establishment within that mind at the subconscious level, of respect for all others. This requires the mental adoption of a moral code which includes 'love' of 'neighbor' with both words properly defined." [3] MacDougald recognizes that churches have attempted to teach this for thousands of years, but their success has been limited because of their lack of understanding of psychology. Thus, theologians have had the right message but insufficient methods to communicate it. Orthodox behavioral science, on the other hand, has generally been opposed to attempts to teach morality on the grounds that it has no scientific basis and may actually be damaging to the individual. MacDougald says of this point of view, "It is generally considered in western psychology that the adoption of a moral code by a criminal is 'ego damaging,' anxiety producing, guilt producing, and therefore increases tension. In short, it's impossible." [3]

Among the assumptions underlying the Yonan Codex program are the following:

1. There are psychological laws regarding human behavior just as there are physical laws pertaining to material things.

2. Understanding and use of these psychological laws (natural laws) leads to behavior that is physiologically and psychologically healthy.

3. Psychopathology is the result of breaking psychological laws.

4. Great minds—prophets, philosophers, and theologians—have described the laws of behavior many times, but the average individual has difficulty discovering these laws for himself. If a man achieves an understanding of the laws of behavior through personal experience, he will choose to follow them because he recognizes that to do so is in his own best interest.

After years of research and preparation a pilot project was started in one of Georgia's maximum security prisons near Reidsville. The program was started in December of 1967 and continued into the spring of 1968. Two convicts, each a psychopathic criminal, one in jail for the fifth time and the other for the second, were individually instructed regarding the Foundation methods. After about twenty hours of training these two, together with two of the Foundation's staff, began instructing 23 convicts in four groups with sessions of two hours a week for 8 weeks. Participation was voluntary. Each participant was given a battery of tests designed to determine his existing attitudes and mental habit patterns. Prisoners were challenged to re-examine attitudes and assumptions they had held for many years, but which had produced nothing but misery for them. Prisoners were taught precise meanings for such words as love, law, neighbor, self, give, spirit, attitude, and authority. They were encouraged to test the effectiveness of these concepts in their daily activities.

All aspects of the experimental program were carefully recorded and documented. Careful records supported by psychological tests and reports; letters from the Georgia Director of Corrections, Mr. Asa Kelley; letters from the prison warden, psychologist, psychiatrist, chaplain, and guards; and testimony from prisoners and their families tell a remarkable story of significant changes in prisoner attitudes. Of the original group of 23, 22 prisoners completed the 8-week, 16-hour course, with all 22 showing constructive change. This was a group of tough convicts—men characterized by their lack of respect for others. The crimes of which they were convicted ranged from multiple murder down to grand larceny, with a record of escapes from less stringent prisons.

The Foundation recognized that parolees could not just be returned to the streets with a few dollars in their pockets. Additional supervision and further training on the outside for several years was considered necessary. Practical training in economics and marriage could not be accomplished in the prison.

A parolee project was established in cooperation with Dougherty County Judicial Circuit. The purpose of this project was to determine whether a trained Yonan Foundation Emotional Maturity instructor could assist county parole offices in determining:

1. Need for confinement of offender.
2. Progress toward changing criminal attitudes in parolees.
3. The fact of rehabilitation.

At the end of seven months a small group (20) had been processed. The Foundation officials are frank to admit that the time is too short and the sample too small for final evaluation, but nevertheless the preliminary results are amazingly good. The method adopted proved 95% accurate in predicting the fact of rehabilitation; that is, which criminals were rehabilitated while on probation and which criminals would require confinement. Continued careful psychological testing showed that most of the participants, approximately 80%, benefited significantly from the training program. Overall the re-arrest of probationers dropped from a norm of 22.5% to 9% for the year involved. Mr. MacDougald states that if further experiments confirm existing trends, the method represents a major breakthrough in the probation, parole, and correction fields.

An unexpected by-product of the Reidsville prison experiment was the discovery that in some cases the method also cured alcoholism and drug addiction. Therefore, the Yonan Foundation established an experimental program for alcoholism in cooperation with the Atlanta Municipal Court. Based on their research into this social problem so frequently related to criminal behavior, the Foundation concluded that alcoholism is a learned behavior pattern which can be unlearned. Tests conducted on several hundred alcoholics found them to be free of psychosis but experiencing conflict between their life experiences and their value systems—a conflict which they seek to avoid by use of alcohol.

It was discovered that alcoholics are different from non-alcoholics in that consumption of limited amounts of alcohol appears to create a craving for additional alcohol, a problem which non-alcoholics do not experience. A second characteristic of chronic alcoholics is that they experience a feeling of greater intelligence and productivity after drinking. The opposite feeling, a feeling of greater stupidity after drinking, is typical for non-alcoholics. The Foundation literature states, "There is considerable conflict in the typical alcoholic's conception of the rules by which man should live and think. All alcoholics, excepting those with considerable contact with Alcoholics Anonymous, exhibit contradictory concepts in the areas of love, punishment, forgiveness, success, and reason." [4]

The alcoholics' program was completely voluntary for court offenders as an alternative to serving full sentence. Participation requires twenty days of residence—the first seven days in the city stockade, and thirteen days at the Yonan-sponsored Guidance Center. The training program in the first experiment was essentially the same as that for criminals and parolees. Approximately one third of the first 61 chronic alcoholics were rehabilitated without confinement (beyond the seven days) and without medical or dietary assistance. This test was then discontinued because it was felt that a much greater percentage of success could be achieved by adding medical and dietary assistance to the Emotional Maturity Instruction program. These more advanced tests are still continuing. The Yonan Codex Foundation is confident that further experiments will confirm initial results, in fact, as they gain greater knowledge of the method, still more sensational results are predicted. All of which is additional validation of some basic assumptions of Dr. Maslow's Third Force theory.

Dr. William Glasser's ideas for an innovative new type of therapy were described in Chapter 14. *Reality Therapy* was first put to the test in the Ventura School for Girls, a California institution for seriously delinquent girls—alcoholics, dope addicts, prostitutes, thieves, and even murderers. Most of these girls had been in and out of juvenile homes and psychiatric treatment, and would have been in jail, but they were less than 21 years of age.

Glasser's objective was to take every girl, no matter how antagonistic, and within six or eight months, rehabilitate her so that, with the assistance of a parole officer, she would stay out of further trouble. The entire staff at the school was involved. Reality and responsibility were concepts the girls could not avoid. They were given vocational training, leisure-time training, and group therapy. Individual therapy was used as required but most of the action occurred in a group setting. Glasser taught the staff to become personally involved with the girls, rather than remaining aloof and authoritarian. Most of the girls had learned to blame their problems on early experiences or unconscious drives or society, but these excuses were no longer permitted. The tenets of Reality Therapy insisted that they accept full responsibility for their behavior.

The group setting is particularly important because patients become involved with one another, soon learning how to confront others in the group with reality and suggest better ways of coping with it.

Dr. Glasser's method proved successful with approximately 80% of the delinquents, a percentage far better than that achieved by other methods, which seldom reach even a 40% rate of success.

If the rate of growth is an indication, *Alcoholics Anonymous* is a highly successful organization. From its modest beginning in 1935 it has grown continuously until today there are over 15,000 A.A. groups in more than 90 countries. The National Council on Alcoholism reports that psychoanalysis has had little success with alcoholics, that alcoholics and psychiatrists have little mutual attraction. A 1969 newspaper article in the *Los Angeles Times* stated that many Los Angeles county judges no longer consign chronic alcoholics to psychiatrists. These judges have found that Alcoholics Anonymous does a far better job, and it is a growing practice among such judges to consign habitual drinkers to A.A.

Alcoholics Anonymous estimates that at least 50% of those who make a serious attempt through the program succeed in controling their problem. The movement recognizes an apparent constitutional difference between alcoholics and average social drinkers. The social drinker is able to control his drinking. The alcoholic is not. One drink invariably leads to another. But the primary emphasis in the A.A. program is on a person's attitude and behavior. Alcoholism is almost invariably accompanied by serious character problems, which are designated as misdirected will power and extreme self-centeredness. Defiance of authority is a common characteristic of many alcoholics. The A.A. program teaches that human instincts are essentially good when properly controlled, but when uncontrolled and misdirected, instincts lead to serious emotional problems. A.A. is a voluntary, self-help teaching program. The study of self is considered a continuing life-long process. The members are taught to be honest with themselves, and when they are it brings about a change in their personalities. Members go through a twelve-step program and the fourth step is to "make a searching and fearless moral inventory of ourselves." They are taught to recognize both their strengths and their weaknesses. It is a program of individual responsibility. Alcoholics are no longer permitted to blame society, their parents, their wives, husbands, or associates. They learn humility and how to live with others. All members of the organization are expected to take responsibility for helping their less fortunate associates. Neophytes soon discover that their problems are not unique; that all alcoholics have suffered fear, envy, resentment, and resistance to honest self-analysis.

"We have found," says the Alcoholics Anonymous manual, "by experience, that we strengthen our own sobriety by offering to share it with others. . . . We have learned that by sharing, by 'giving away' our sobriety, our own ability to stay sober is reinforced."

The *Synanon Foundation* is the brain child of Charles Dederich. It is a self-help program for drug addicts. Dederich, who had no professional training in psychology, got many of his ideas from his own personal experience with Alcoholics Anonymous. Tom Patten, a member of the Synanon organization says, "We do not begin with a presumption of sickness, as have virtually all psychological orientations since Freud. Instead, at Synanon we assume that people behave badly not because they are ill, or ill-willed, but because they are stupid. . . . Drug addicts are much more addicted to stupid ways of thinking and acting than they are to drugs." [5]

It is a voluntary program. Addicts come of their own free will and may leave any time they wish, but generally more than half of those who stay are cured. This is a success record far superior to that of orthodox psychiatry and psychology. The program depends almost entirely upon ex-addicts convincing the user that he has the ability to break the habit. In the first phase, which may take about a year, the new member lives in one of Synanon's residence buildings. The drug habit is kicked "cold turkey" and in the supporting atmosphere of the home. The patient learns to assume responsibility, first by doing simple tasks at Synanon. Three nights each week all members of the home meet together for group discussion or therapy. The method is direct confrontation. At this time everyone is given full opportunity to speak his mind. What they say is examined carefully by the rest of the group. Complete honesty and reality are demanded.

Most addicts have never had a friendly home environment, and this is one of the secrets of Synanon's success. The members find themselves with a group that acts as brother, sister, father, and mother. The group cares about each individual. The new member gradually learns to accept and abide by rules and schedules, and to accept more and more responsibility for his own life.

In the second stage, members take jobs outside of Synanon but return "home" each night. In the third stage, they live and work outside of Synanon and become responsible members of the community. Maslow personally sat in on some of Synanon's group sessions and was highly impressed by what he saw. "In this society," he wrote, "the contempt for social workers, psychiatrists, and other 'experts' is thick and heavy. There is a total mistrust and hatred and sometimes fear of 'mere' book knowledge, of people with degrees, of people who are certified as knowing but who, in fact, know nothing. . . . As nearly as I can make out, the Synanon type of treatment cures many of its addicts, while our whole apparatus of hospitals, physicians, police, prisons, psychiatrists and social workers cures practically none." [6]

Daytop Village on Staten Island is another successful drug addiction center. David Deitch, former executive director, reports, "The addicts are 'taught' to grow up—taught responsibility." [7] He reports records for a period of 18 months which show that 84% of those who stay at Daytop for one month will sooner or later remain to get well. The program, like Synanon, is voluntary and approximately 60% of those who enter remain. It takes 18 to 24 months to help the inmates develop a new personality—one "starkly different from that of the dope fiend who entered." [7]

Mr. Deitch describes the attitude of Daytop's group therapy in the following words, "I will relate to you in a manner that befits the dignity of man. It means that I refuse to act as though you are fragile, or crippled, or damned. I will, instead, regard you as capable of fulfilling your aspirations, and I will expect you to try to be productive, and to reduce, rather than to rationalize, your failures." [8]

Effren E. Ramirez, M.D., is a psychiatrist who has worked for many years to solve the problems of drug addiction. His approach is quite different from orthodox psychiatry because he places his entire stress on rebuilding the addict's character. He achieved a remarkable record of success in his Puerto Rican treatment center. Of 124 addicts treated, only seven returned to drugs within three and one half years after treatment. This is a relapse rate of 5.6%, compared with an estimated average 92% failure for addicts treated in federal institutions. "When I began working with addicts nine years ago," says Dr. Ramirez, "I was told that addiction is a chronic, incurable disease. I no longer believe that. Instead, I am convinced that the addiction can be cured. I am also convinced that there is no such thing as purely physiologic addiction and that the addict's problem results from a fundamental but treatable character disorder. The typical addict has a weak sense of responsibility, little commitment to anyone or anything. His life is dismally disorganized and he can't seem to learn from his failures.

He shows poor motivation to be cured, and the current belief that addiction is physiological just gives the addict another excuse for saying, 'I can't help myself.' . . . I believe everyone wants to become a complete human being. But addicts have not built a psychological structure for following through on desires." [9]

Dr. Ramirez, like Synanon and Daytop, relies upon ex-addicts to help other addicts. Group confrontation is an important part of the program, and the full rehabilitation job takes from two to three years to complete.

CHAPTER 16

Education and Personal Potential

Dr. Maslow and other Third Force theorists have had a significant impact on education at all levels. A considerable number of interesting educational experiments were examined for possible inclusion in this chapter. The problem is that educational objectives are not easily defined or measured. Results do not always appear immediately. Perhaps the following examples will indicate important new trends.

Most discussions of human potential start with a reference to William James (1842–1910), one of the great names in American Psychology. James considered the discovery of untapped human potential the most important discovery of his era. "I have no doubt whatever," he said, "that most people live whether physically, intellectually, or morally, in a very restricted circle of their potential being . . . the so-called 'normal man' of commerce, so to speak, the healthy Philistine, is a mere extract from the potentially realizable individual he represents, and we all have reservoirs of life to draw upon of which we do not dream." [1] At another time he said, "Compared to what we ought to be, we are only half awake. Our fires are dampened, our drafts are checked. We are making use of only a small part of our mental and physical resources." [1] Not only did William James believe that the average man was utilizing only about 10% of his potential, but also that this unused potential could be developed by the use of proper techniques—"men can alter their lives by altering their minds."

Interest in human potential waned after William James. Psychologists were more concerned with psychopathology than psychological health. In 1954 Gardner Murphy published *Human Potentialities*. This along with the work of Maslow, Carl Rogers, Erich Fromm, and others focused attention once again on man's undeveloped resources. A direct outgrowth of this new trend was the establishment of Esalen Institute at Big Sur, California. By the end of 1969 more than ninety growth centers were scattered across the nation.

Herbert Otto, Ph.D., is a social psychologist and former director of the Human Potentialities Research Project at the University of Utah. He has pioneered in developing many effective methods to develop human potential.[2] When he announced the opening of the National Center for the Exploration of Human Potential, La Jolla, California in 1967, he said, "The topic of human potentialities has for the last fifty years, been almost totally ignored as a discrete focus of research activities by workers in the social and behavioral sciences . . . all that one finds are individual pioneers conducting limited studies under extremely limited conditions. . . ." [3] He conducted experimental classes at the University of Utah with what he referred to as "healthy, well-functioning individuals." These adult evening classes were entitled "Developing Your Personal Potential." The prospectus stated: "This program is designed to help you discover capacities, strengths, talents, and abilities which you have but which you may not be aware of or using fully. Emphasis is on discovering your potentialities and developing them, leading to more vital, creative, satisfying living and productivity." [4]

Dr. Otto discovered through the experimental classes and groups that the most productive techniques were those which emphasized people's positive experiences and abilities—concentrated on their strengths rather than their weaknesses. Dwelling on past failures was not only very productive, but sometimes destructive. He states, "Everyone is starved for the deserved recognition and praise which should come with a job well done. In our pathology and problem-centered culture, the emphasis is continually on the deficiences, the shortcomings, the mistakes, and the in-adequacies of people. Yet psychological tests with children have clearly revealed that when tired children were given a word of praise or commen-dation, an upward surge of new energy was evident. (An endless number of cases can be cited where the praise and encouragement of the child by his teacher has significantly influenced his course and development in life.) Conversely, when children were criticized or discouraged, their available physical energy declined dramatically."

"As the noted psychologist Erik Erikson has pointed out, the ego iden-tity of children 'gains real strength only from whole-hearted and consistent recognition of real accomplishment.' This also applies to adults. A consid-erable number of psychological studies indicate that if adult subjects in experiments are rewarded by praise and commendation, their perform-ance significantly improves as judged by themselves and by others, and gains are evident in leadership, participation, and self confidence. . . ." [2] Prior to his work at the University of Utah, Otto was a director of a mental health and education program at the University of Georgia and conducted a number of workshops with educators. He discovered a destructive pat-tern of critical behavior. "Teachers repeatedly mentioned with great bit-terness, 'no one ever tells me when I do a good job, but when I make a mistake I hear plenty.' During workshops with school administrators a principal said, 'All I get is criticism from teachers and parents; they never notice my accomplishments.' A superintendent remarked, 'The principals remember when I have last had kind words about anything I have done.' Members of the Board of Education said, 'The parents and everybody else runs to us with their complaints. We volunteer our time and energy but nobody ever thanks us for what we do.' Completing the cycle, in group discussions with parents the following or similar comments were often heard, 'We try hard to raise our children right and to help them with their schoolwork, but never hear a kind word of appreciation for it.'" [2]

Dr. Otto has developed and tested an impressive list of group tech-niques to help people to identify and enhance their capabilities. His numerous case histories reveal some remarkable personality changes. For example: Mrs. R., age 37, was the first member of a group to be "strength bombarded." "Strength bombardment" is a procedure which begins with a group member stating what he thinks his own personality strengths are. Then members of the group offer what *they* see as the individual's strengths. Mrs. R. appeared very confident when listing her own strengths, but, as soon as the group started explaining their perception of her strengths, she became noticeably ill at ease. In a very short time she suggested that everyone stop talking about her; she felt that the group had spent enough time with her and was bored and wanted to get on to something else. The group did not seem bored to one of the leaders, who said so. He also suggested that maybe it was Mrs. R. who was uncomfortable and wanted the group to get on to someone else. Mrs. R. vehemently denied the implication, and the group went on, but now with a seeming reluctance. Later Mrs. R. was heard to remark that she had checked with several of the group members after the meeting, and that they had been bored; she also said she thought the leader was "pushy."

When Mrs. R. returned to class the following week she told the group that she thought the "strength bombardment" experience had changed her life. She said she had gone home very angry with the "pushy" leader, but feeling that something inside her had been jarred loose. She had felt ambivalent as the group had zeroed in on her. She wanted help but didn't feel that they knew enough to help her. She wanted to hear good things about herself, but was afraid to for fear she would then be expected to *do* something. She reported that she found herself doing and saying things she had never done before. She had gone home and asked her husband to sit down and talk with her, and they had talked together for over an hour. She said that, although she had been married for 12 years, that was the first time she had seen him as an individual. They had really communicated. She told him of her feeling of being pushed, and he said he had never been able to reach her nor to help her because she was so touchy about being pushed. She realized that this had been a problem with her ever since childhood, one that made her feel isolated and "picked on." She had frequently complained that no one wanted to help or cooperate with her, but she now realized that when they had tried, she withdrew from them because she felt "pushed."

Dr. Otto refers to the idea of the study of healthy individuals as indispensable to the understanding of man and sees as the most challenging question of today: "How can we help man to develop and utilize that latent 90% of his potential? . . . In the behavioral sciences and particularly psychology, indications are that we are on the threshold of a major breakthrough." [5] Dr. Otto also conducts classes and group experiences in developing personal potential at U.C.L.A. and several other universities.

Otto calls attention to the work of Dr. W. Ross Adey and Associates at the UCLA Space Biology Laboratory of the Brain Research Institute. Dr. Adey says, "The ultimate creative capacity of the brain may be, for all practical purposes, infinite." [4]

Otto also refers to a Russian publication dated November, 1964, reporting the work of Vasili Davydov of the Moscow Institute of Psychology. A report headed "Inexhaustible Brain Potential" states, "The latest findings in anthropology, psychology, logic, and physiology show that the potential of the human mind is very great indeed. 'As soon as modern science gave us some understanding of the structure and work of the human brain we were struck by its enormous reserve capacity,' writes Ivan Yefremov, eminent Soviet scholar and writer. 'Man, under average conditions of work and life uses only a small part of his thinking equipment. . . . If we were able to force our brain to work at only half its capacity we could, without any difficulty whatever, learn forty languages, memorize the large Soviet Encyclopedia from cover to cover, and complete the required courses of dozens of colleges.' The statement is hardly an exaggeration. It is the generally accepted theoretical view of man's potentiality. How can we tap this gigantic potential? It is a vague and very complex problem with many ramifications." [5]

John K. Boyle, in his 4-day resident seminar, *Executive Power,* has taught thousands of executives, professional men, and their wives how to develop their latent potential. Boyle describes the doctrine of total personal responsibility and quotes William James, "Man alone, of all the creatures of earth, can change his own pattern, man alone is architect of his destiny." "Change and growth," says Boyle, "are the natural state of man. They are absolutely necessary for a satisfying, healthy, and mature life. Any person resisting this flow, and seeking a static life, is inviting a pathological condition." [6]

When the course was started in 1957, Mr. Boyle intended to teach the poor and the social misfits. He soon discovered that, although his fees were then nominal, these men were not interested in the program. The men who sought his advice were already successful, but wanted to improve. The name of the organization was changed to Institute for Executive Research.

The program is based on extensive research and John Boyle's personal discovery that man can change. He says of his early life, "I was a failure in nearly every possible way." In a desperate attempt to create a new way of life, he studied the work of William James, Jung, Emerson, Pavlov, Assagioli, Gardner Murphy, and many others. He then spent many months on an ambitious project—interviewing hundreds of successful business men to discover a possible common denominator of success in personal effectiveness. These ideas and the influence of his wife, Helen, a trained psychotherapist, changed his life from failure to success.

Dr. James Fadiman, working with Dr. Richard Katz on a new book, *Transformations: The Meaning of Personal Growth,* describes the Executive Power Seminar as, "Unusually successful." [7] Primary emphasis of the course is on the achievement of practical results and increased effectiveness. A recent survey of seminar graduates reveals that, for those who graduated more than a year ago, incomes were up an average of 142%. More recent graduates (less than one year since completion of the course) reported a 34% average increase in income. A number of stockbrokers and insurance counselors reported income increases of two or three hundred percent within two years. Wives are encouraged to take the course with their husbands, and they report an increased ability to relax and enjoy life, a better understanding of children, and dramatic improvements in solving family problems. Nearly all graduates find the course improves their relationships with others, especially with their mates and children. The benefit most often mentioned, for both men and women, is "self assurance with growth toward maturity."

James Newman, a former instructor and sales manager for Executive Dynamics, formed his own organization in 1961. He calls his seminar PACE (Personal and Company Effectiveness). He teaches that most adults have a distorted perception of themselves and others—a poor perception of reality—usually acquired in their childhood. Fortunately, the result is not irrevocable. He has taught thousands of executives and their wives that they have the ability to change their habits and personalities. Newman calls the PACE philosophy "a concept of goal-directed responsibility. . . . as a man thinks, he is." In addition to adult courses Newman founded the PACE Foundation to teach self-actualization concepts to high-school seniors, college freshmen, and sophomores. These one-week conferences have been highly successful in developing positive attitudes in young people.

Spring Realty Corporation offers an example of the power of the ideas taught by men like James Newman and John Boyle. It started in 1963 when Sid Syvertson and Jim Guillet and their wives attended a PACE Seminar. Here they learned that the average individual is only using a small percentage of his potential. They learned the importance of setting worthwhile goals and working to achieve them. They discovered how they had acquired bad habits and negative thinking in their youth and how to overcome these subconscious blocks to growth. They learned that the individual could take responsibilities for his own future. They studied basic principles of human relations: how to understand and appreciate other people's point of view, how to communicate, creativity, etc. Shortly after the seminar Sid and Jim formed Spring Realty, Inc. With Sid as president, they proceeded to apply the principles they had learned. They presented the PACE principles to each new employee in a manual and held frequent training meetings. Setting standards most people would think too high to be practical, Spring has grown at a phenomenal rate until today it is one of the top ranking realty firms in California. The average salesman starting with Spring had been earning about $7,000 or $8,000 a year. After a year of training and experience the average man earns $15,000 annually.

"Respect for the human dignity of the individual," says President Syvertson, "is a basic corporate policy." Coupled with this respect for people is a determination to give outstanding service. The management insists on scrupulous honesty in all transactions. Prospective buyers are discouraged from buying houses too expensive for their income.

1966 was a bad year for real estate. Estimates of closures of California firms were as high as 40%. Spring Realty took the tight market in stride and continued to grow and prosper. Both partners credit their success and enthusiasm to the ideas they learned at the PACE Seminar.

Dr. William Glasser now devotes most of his energy toward preventing delinquency before it occurs. His years of experience with delinquent girls and the mentally ill convinced the Doctor that education was the key to sound human functioning. "We will never succeed in patching people up," he says, "we must get them responsibly involved from early childhood in an educational system in which they can succeed enough to function successfully in our society." [8]

Glasser's book *Schools Without Failure* describes the application of the principles of Reality Therapy to public education. He, like Maslow, objects to the deterministic point of view which has been so prevalent in orthodox behavioral science. He writes, "I do not accept the rationalization of failure commonly accepted today, that these young people are products of a social situation that precludes success. Blaming their failure upon their homes, their communities, their culture, their background, their race, or their poverty is a dead end for two reasons: 1. it removes personal responsibility for failure, and 2. it does not recognize that success is potentially open to all young people." [8]

Children have two basic needs—the need for love and the need for self-worth. This might also be described as the single need for identity. He defines love as it applies to young children as social responsibility. Children need to "learn to be responsible for each other, to care for each other, and to help each other, not only for the sake of others, but for their own sake . . ." [8]

The need for self-worth, to feel worthwhile, is intimately related to the concept of love. If a child does not feel worthwhile he cannot feel loved, and the best way to feel worthwhile is to be worthwhile. Children need to experience success early in life, but the typical American public school is designed for failure. Those who experience only failure tend to give up, to stop trying; they lose motivation. Dr. Glasser estimates that in the average secondary school over 50% of the students are learning very little, and this happens even to talented children from good homes. The situation in central city slum areas is even worse—the majority here become failure oriented. The child who is failure oriented becomes a problem for his school and for society. These children are the reservoir from which springs delinquency. Dr. Glasser observed that the most common characteristic of delinquent girls was hopelessness. They have no hope for the future. They may be intelligent and physically attractive, but because they have never or seldom experienced success, they cannot imagine that they will succeed in the future.

The solution is to provide schools where success is not only possible, but probable. The necessary ingredients are involvement, relevance, and a problem-solving approach. Glasser found again and again in questioning school children that they did not see much value in most of the material they were expected to learn. "In addition to reading, the most important subject in elementary schools," he writes, "we must attempt to relate every subject taught—arithmetic, social studies, science, health, and even spelling and handwriting—to something that the children do in their own lives outside of school. *When relevance is absent from the curriculum, children do not gain the motivation to learn.*" [8]

The method which proved most effective in accomplishing these objectives was classroom group discussion. It was found that when the children were arranged in a circle with the teacher part of the circle, exciting things happened. Through skillful questioning, which requires special training, teachers can encourage their children to think for themselves, to learn to solve problems, to develop social consciousness and a feeling of self-worth. The emphasis is on the present and the future, not past failures. The Doctor found two questions helped the children to analyze their own behavior. The first "What are you doing?" and the second, "and does it help?" This opens the door for an examination of alternate approaches. The child is given choices; this teaches him responsibility. But once he has made a choice he is expected to follow through without excuses; this teaches him discipline. Glasser does not believe in corporal punishment, but he does not believe in permissiveness, either. When their choices are wrong, they must be prepared to accept the consequences. "They may choose to disobey the rules; this choice is open to all. But they then have to accept the consequences of their choice. . . . Neither school nor therapist should attempt to manipulate the world so that the child does not suffer the reasonable consequences of his behavior." [8]

Children must be given a certain degree of freedom. Only thus can they learn responsibility. But, it is a freedom to fail as well as succeed. The important thing is that they taste enough success to become motivated to do more. It is a philosophy of personal responsibility. "In helping children we must work to make them understand that they are responsible for filling their needs . . . without hard work and personal discipline students will fail no matter how much we improve schools." [8]

Dr. Glasser is opposed to lowering standards to insure success. He tells about his experience as a consultant to an Upward Bound Program at UCLA. The program was designed to take culturally deprived young people and, through special training, prepare them for higher education. The program was in difficulty when Glasser was called in. He found the program based on the assumptions of orthodox sociology. It was assumed that, because these children had experienced little but failure and punishment and had great difficulty obeying rules, what was needed was "a permissive environment with few rules and little enforcement." [8] The problem with this approach, says Glasser, is the failure to understand "that the children have not yet learned to behave in a permissive environment in ways that will be beneficial to them." [8] He recommended reasonable rules, firmly enforced, and extensive utilization of the group problem-solving approach. "Those who would completely relax rules are so anxious to please 'deprived' children that they fail to understand that firm, fair standards of discipline mean that we care; lax standards are interpreted by those who need firm standards as lack of interest." [8]

One highly successful demonstration of Dr. Glasser's ideas was carried out in Pershing Elementary School (600 students) near Sacramento. Mr. Donald O'Donnel, principal of the school, heard Glasser speak in 1962 and talked to the doctor about his own conviction that warm personal involvement between students and teachers was a key to educational success. Glasser agreed to work as a consultant with Pershing School, and described this as "one of the most innovative and important elementary-school programs in the country." [8]

Two special teaching positions were created: one to direct a program for educationally handicapped children in the first three grades and the other to concentrate on children with reading problems. An important assumption of the teaching program was that it is in the first three grades that children's problems need to be solved. It is in these early years that children need to taste success rather than continued failure. In contrast to most conventional approaches to problem children, the extra teacher did not remove these students from their classroom, but worked with them in special groups in the same classroom. The special teacher, Mr. Maxwell, was subordinate to the regular classroom teacher—she was in charge, and she directed his participation in her class. The remedial specialist also used this approach, working with small groups of students in their regular classroom. This unique idea of having two extra teachers on call, as needed by the various full-time teachers, proved stimulating and encouraging to the entire faculty. Dr. Glasser says of this experiment, "In the imaginative program at Pershing, . . . three cornerstones of education—involvement, relevance, and thinking—are a reality not an idea. Available to any school that wants to implement them, the program has given the children an educational experience equaled by few public or private schools in America." [8]

Stanley Coopersmith, Ph.D. is a psychologist at the University of California at Davis and a former student under Dr. Maslow at Brandeis University. His research is particularly significant because it too emphasizes healthy behavior rather than psychopathology and examines in depth one of Maslow's basic needs, self-esteem. Dr. Coopersmith's research consisted of a six-year study of ten to twelve year old boys from middle-class families. The attitudes of the children were carefully determined by a variety of research techniques, and the training methods of the parents, especially the mothers, were carefully analyzed.

The research findings published in 1967 in the book entitled *The Antecedents of Self-Esteem* challenged some long-cherished concepts of Freudian psychoanalytical theory. Coopersmith defines self-esteem as follows: "The self evaluation which the individual makes and customarily maintains with regard to himself; it expresses an attitude of approval or disapproval, and indicates the extent to which the individual believes himself to be capable, significant, successful, and worthy." [9]

Coopersmith found high self-esteem individuals to be characteristically more independent, creative, confident in their own judgment and ideas, courageous, socially independent (self-determining), psychologically stable, less anxious, and more success oriented. Such individuals see themselves as competent and have high expectations for the future which generally result in greater motivation. Persons with high self-esteem are generally happier and more effective in their daily life than those with low self-esteem. Low self-esteem individuals lack trust in themselves and are reluctant to express themselves in a group, especially if their ideas are new or creative. They tend to listen rather than participate, are self-conscious and self-preoccupied. They are far less successful in interpersonal relationships and frequently less active in social, civic, and political affairs. "Persons who seek psychological help," writes Coopersmith, "frequently acknowledge that they suffer from feelings of inadequacy and unworthiness. These people see themselves as helpless and inferior—incapable of improving their situations and lacking the inner resources to tolerate or reduce the anxiety readily aroused by everyday events and stress. Clinicians observe that persons who are plagued by doubts of their worthiness can neither give nor receive love, apparently fearing that the exposure that comes with intimacy will reveal their inadequacies and cause them to be rejected. They thus avoid closeness in their relationships and feel isolated as a consequence." [9]

An interesting discovery was that some rather competent people had low self-esteem, while others with considerable less competence had relatively high self-esteem. The explanation Coopersmith gives is that self-esteem is related to expectations. Some people have unreasonably high expectations relative to their actual performance, and even though their performance might be good in the eyes of others, it is inadequate in their own eyes. Not too surprisingly, high self-esteem children usually had high self-esteem parents, but the relationship was not invariable.

The typical parents of high self-esteem boys were found to be more loving and attentive toward their children, but also more demanding and specific in the rules of behavior. Parents of high self-esteem children have conveyed to their children high demands for academic performance. Although they establish rather specific rules and limits, they are also more tolerant of the children's discussing and even challenging these limits.

Parents of low-esteem children established few or poorly defined rules, and their methods of control tended to be harsh and autocratic. The report describes the less successful parents as follows: "The characteristic actions of rejecting parents stand in sharp distinction to the warmth and approval expressed by those more accepting in nature. These parents are hostile, cold and disapproving of their child and regard him as an intrusive, value-less or even negative object. They express their rejection by neglecting their child and by a callous indifference to his requests, needs, or aspirations. He is depreciated and treated as a burden who must be borne—an affliction and legal responsibility rather than a valued and desirable trust. . . . A more vigorous form of rejection results in overt and vigorous manifestations of hostility, such as open declarations of dislike, harsh and unwarranted punishment, and deprivation of physical necessities and social attention. Both passive and active forms of rejection express disinterest, disapproval, and distaste for the child." [9]

Low self-esteem parents don't expect very much from their children, and their negative expectations are generally fulfilled. Low self-esteem parents are characteristically dominating, and their tendency toward punishment results in children with low self-esteem. The research does not reveal any significant correlation between the children's self-esteem and the social status of their parents. High self-esteem children are just as apt to come from parents of modest social status as they are from more well-to-do families. Nor are families of high self-esteem children always tranquil, harmonious, and open minded. These families have a tendency toward independence, open dissent, and disagreement. Such parents, says Coopersmith, tend to have firm convictions, frequent and often strong verbal exchanges, and are capable and ready to assume leadership. They will not tolerate casual or disrespectful treatment.

Dr. Coopersmith is highly critical of permissive child training. He says, "The concept of permissiveness received its most forceful advocacy by early adherents of psychoanalytic theory. They argued that children would develop into better adjusted and more secure adults if they were reared under open flexible schedules that were geared to their needs. They proposed that the use of such schedules would result in more immediate gratification and relief and, hence, provide the child with a sense of trust in himself and confidence in others . . . the advocates of permissive rearing pointed to the adverse effects of repressive treatment and concluded that non-restricted, self demand procedures would permit greater self expression and self trust. This uncritical extension of psychoanalytical theory was based on the implicit assumption that greater impulse expression and gratification was associated with more favorable development, greater happiness, and better adaptation. . . . The general notions of family democracy and permissiveness failed to consider that children have less knowledge and foresight than their parents, that expressions based on ignorance tend to be aimless, and that parents are ultimately responsible for the conduct of their young children.

"Authority was equated with authoritarianism, discipline was associated with punishment and restrictions were thought to indicate rejection.

"From the results obtained in this study, it appears that parents who accepted this *redefinition* were not very confident of their own beliefs and were also more likely to produce anxious rather than confident children. . . . It appears that the requirements for maintaining and protecting the child and reconciling the needs of the various members of the family make some (minimum) regulations and restrictions inevitable. To call parents who establish such regulations rejecting, undemocratic, or punitive, is to disregard the realities of child rearing. . . . the parents of children with high self-esteem are significantly less permissive than are the parents of children with less self-esteem." [9]

Character Education

Early advocates of public education took moral education for granted. John Dewey, for example, said in 1916, "It is a commonplace of educational theory that establishment of character is a comprehensive aim of school instruction and discipline."

Two years later the Commission on Reorganization of Secondary Education, appointed by the National Educational Association, issued an historic statement regarding the goals of public education. The statement has since been identified as the "Seven Cardinal Principles of Education." The principles are: 1. Health, 2. Command of fundamental processes, 3. Worthy home membership, 4. Vocation, 5. Citizenship, 6. Worthy use of leisure, 7. Ethical character. But the Freudian-Behavioristic point of view had a major influence in down-grading the emphasis on character development in the United States educational system. Influenced by this point of view, John Dewey himself became far less enthusiastic about moral instruction. Dr. Benjamin Wood, director of the Bureau of Collegiate Educational Research at Columbia University, referred to the changed emphasis as, "the lamentable disengagement of American Education from its indispensable role in the moral ethical realm. . . ." [10] Another professional educator, writing for the *Indiana Social Studies Quarterly* in 1965, said, "Probably the biggest change between 1900 and 1950 was that social studies came to be seen as primarily serving a socializing function as opposed to the earlier 'transmission of cultural heritage' role." [11]

Sigmund Freud discouraged moral education because of his conviction that mental illness was the result of imposed moral standards, too high for man's animal nature. Many behaviorists were equally vehement in their opposition to "fixed moral values" in a society where human nature was constantly changing and right and wrong had no scientific basis. Dr. Viktor Frankl, an outspoken critic of such moral relativism said, "Education which is still based on the homeostasis theory, avoids confronting young people with ideals and values so that as few demands as possible may be imposed on them." [12]

A national survey of the state of moral instruction in public schools was conducted for the California State Department of Education in 1969. Officials in each state were asked whether their state department of education had prepared guidelines for moral instruction to be used by the schools in that state. Twenty-eight states replied that they had neither guidelines nor any committees studying the issue.

An earlier survey by the Greater Cleveland Educational Research Council concluded that "The nation's schools have no grand design for a kindergarten-through-twelfth grade curriculum to develop sound realistic judgment in social matters. In fact the void in this vital area has for over a decade constituted an educational scandal." [13] And the National Educational Association found through a national questionnaire to classroom teachers, that approximately 52% of the teachers responding believed that not enough emphasis is placed on the teaching of character in the schools.

Abraham Maslow's position in this controversial aspect of public education is quite explicit. "I want to demonstrate that spiritual values have naturalistic meaning, that they are not the exclusive possession of organized churches, that they do not need supernatural concepts to validate them, that they are well within the jurisdiction of a suitably enlarged science, and that, therefore, they are the general responsibility of all mankind. If all of this is so, then we shall have to reevaluate the possible place of spiritual and moral values in education. For, if these values are not exclusively identified with churches, then teaching values in the schools need not breach the wall between church and state." [14]

American Viewpoint,. Inc., a New York based non-profit corporation, has been interested in character education since 1922. The organization believes that since ethical principles have been developed through centuries of trial and error—"hammered out on the anvil of practical experience" —they are a proper subject for public education without violating the principle of separation of state and religion. The President of American Viewpoint since 1949 has been Herbert C. Mayer, a former college president and specialist in higher education for the U.S. Office of Education. He holds a master's degree in psychology and an Ed.D. in educational philosophy from Harvard Graduate School of Education. Under Dr. Mayer's direction the organization conducted extensive research into the causes of delinquency. The conclusions were that "there is a very low correlation between delinquency and poverty, or housing, or mixed population groups. Environment seems to have far less influence than is generally assumed. The fact is that some rates of delinquency have been high in areas where the environment would be considered favorable to good behavior and very low in some cases where surroundings would be judged detrimental. It's not the environment, but the attitude of the person toward his surroundings that determines his ideals and his behavior." [15]

These research findings were supported by the previous work of Bernard Lander in Baltimore, Maryland, and the famous husband and wife team, Drs. Sheldon and Eleanor Glueck, at Harvard University. The Gluecks, who are noted for their many years of research into crime and delinquency, state, "In ultimate analysis prevention of delinquent careers is dependent on something more specific than the manipulation of general cultural environment. It entails the structuring of integrated personality and wholesome character during the first formative years of life." [16]

Dr. Mayer is highly critical of the common idea that values are caught, but can't be taught. He believes that this erroneous idea is a major cause of failure, and that to be successful, schools need to teach values directly and systematically. The American Viewpoint "Good American" program has been developed and tested in the public-school system of Ossining, New York since 1959. The program does not call for special courses in ethics, however, but is incorporated into the already existing social studies. Indoctrination is carefully avoided. Teachers are taught to help the children think moral concepts through and test them in their everyday living. At the same time children are encouraged to gain inspiration from the study of the lives of great men. The program's teachers' manual lists and identifies 22 character values. This list was developed from a national inquiry to outstanding educators, philosophers, theologians, and others. It includes such values as conservation, courage, personal efficiency, freedom, health, honesty, initiative, perserverance, reliability, cooperation, courtesy, friendliness, respect, tolerance, and understanding. The Ossining schools developed a systematic schedule to be sure that each child in the system was exposed to these value concepts at some time during his first six years. The educator found that timing was very important. Some of the values depend upon abstract ideas, and needed to be introduced at a proper age. The teaching manual developed in Ossining contains the following passage which gives insight into the method.

"Extolling a virtue is interesting and perhaps useful in understanding more about people, but it ends short of putting it to work. How can a teacher carry the teaching process to a real result? A discussion can enumerate the things that can be done or not done, as a means of setting up a simple set of goals to be achieved. This may result in a class code of action agreed upon as an ideal to be striven for, or in a set of rules the class adopts for carrying on its own activities in the light of a given value. As a step toward practical action, it may involve role playing in a number of situations which the class recognizes in its discussion. It may result in a set of actions agreed upon for a particular activity on the playground. It may even list those things which children ought to do or ought not to do in their free play or at home.

"A first and most important part of putting an idea into action is to set a practical goal toward which to work as a basis for judging oneself. A second step is the checking to determine whether or not individuals have lived up to their objective. Achievement can help fix a pattern of action and even failure can kindle renewed zeal to live up to the ideal. Stock taking of this kind can be helpful in the process and it may require going back over some of the previous steps noted in the process of teaching. Certainly there should be constant friendly review and repetition of ideas and actions until they do take some form of expression in action. Even repeated failures can be used by good teaching to reveal the difficulty of a problem and help a child try again until he does achieve his goal. In this process, the study of people, that is, biography, is particularly helpful." [16]

At one time a religious group challenged the Ossining program on the basis that it was state interference with religion. The school superintendent invited the parents to study the program in greater detail and observe what was actually going on in the classroom. When this had been done the group withdrew its objections.

American Viewpoint admits that they have had difficulty developing objective methods to measure the results of the program. If the enthusiasm of teachers, school administrators, parents, and children is any indication, the program is a success. On one occasion when supervision was interrupted by the death of a staff member, a teacher committee asked the superintendent of schools for his consent to go ahead with the administration of the character-education program. More than 100 Eastern schools and school districts have utilized the American Viewpoint Citizenship Teaching Manual to improve their own educational programs.

Mrs. Virginia Trevitt taught 9th grade students at the high school in Colton, California. She was not satisfied with the results she was getting. Her students were restless and careless; some of them carried knives; others, although still in their early teens, were very bitter. Twenty percent of them were Mexican Americans. Few were satisfied with the world they knew, and none of them had been challenged to the limits of their capacity. Mrs. Trevitt prepared a course of study dealing with character development. The program was accepted by the Board of Education, and she taught it to all incoming freshmen five days a week for three years. Among the aims of the course were "to create a new type of student who sees education as relevant to the needs of the world. To equip the individual with the moral qualities needed to make his best contribution to his generation." [17]

She provoked heated discussions by asking pointed questions about daily living and encouraged her students to test some of the ideas they developed in their daily activities. She gave these young people a chance to rediscover the ideals of American democracy—ideals which, when understood and lived, give a blueprint for greatness.

Contrary to ideas currently popular about young people, Mrs. Trevitt found that the majority of her students responded to the challenge. They were excited about the opportunity to discuss moral concepts. "Students enjoy trying things out," Mrs. Trevitt says, "to see if they will work. It is exciting to them to discover by trial that honesty is not only 'the best policy' but that it works." [17] The changes which resulted from the program were sometimes spectacular. Here are some typical case histories:

"Bob was a track star. He was also a sentimentalist. He had successfully appropriated the track suit which, he believed, had brought him several victories. It had some magic attached to it, and he felt he could not risk being issued a new one each time a competition arose. In the second semester, when the experiments with honesty were tried, Bob thought about the track suit. When small deviations were discussed in relation to larger forms of corruption and graft in the nation, Bob decided that the principle of honesty was what counted and not the legal size or consequence of the deed. He could understand that the national debt could be reduced if every citizen were honest. He could understand, also, that theft from a tax-supported institution was like robbing his parents. He returned the track suit which he had persuaded himself was his own. This action brought him new integrity and paved the way for a decision to be an honest citizen." [17]

"John had the appearance of a typical American boy. At first he looked upon this kind of orientation with skepticism. School bored him. He said he intended to quit when he became sixteen. He came from a home of poverty and disorder. His parents both drank and gambled. He hated his little brothers for whose care he was often responsible. John finally became interested in the change in some of his classmates. He was secretly fascinated by the idea that if he wanted to see things different, the place to start was with himself. Quietly, off the record, John began to try the experiment of changing his ways at home. He organized his little brothers into a clean-up brigade. They worked together like Trojans to clear debris from their unkempt yard. John marked off a crude basketball court. He trained his young team to play the game and grew quite proud of them. This was a change from the old wrangling and punishments. Next he invaded the home and taught the little brothers to make their beds. One night he was honest with his parents about all the bitterness he felt toward them. He apologized. He said he wanted to stop being critical and rebellious so he could help his family. His mother told me later, confidentially, 'That night his father and I both wept.' The rewarding result was that the mother and father stopped drinking and gambling. They painted their house, inside and out. The community was astonished. John's grades went up. Three years later he graduated from high school and entered one of our best colleges. He graduated from that college, served in the Air Force and is now a businessman with a home and family of his own." [17]

"Pedro belonged to a gang where knife fights were the popular sport. He was handsome, arrogant, and cynical. His father ran a pool hall and drank too much. His mother had her own crowd and family life was catch-as-catch can. One day from some new friends Pedro got the idea of using his love of adventure constructively. They convinced him that there was a need for his dare and that it would take a real fight to give his Mexican people a place in the sun. The right fight! He decided to give up his knife and quit the gang. He knew that the old crowd might attack him, but now he had friends he could trust. Finally, he talked to his father and admitted he'd been in trouble with the police. There had been women and liquor. He had decided that all this had to go. He'd hated his mother and father for making his home a battleground. He apologized for his resentment, and had learned that bitterness only led to bloodshed. He told his father he wanted to work with him to clean up the community. . . . The new direction Pedro had taken manifestly affected his parents. They went back to the church of their faith. They stopped drinking. The father sold the pool hall and built a hardware store where his sons could work with him after school. Two years after Pedro had made his new start the family was considered one of the most responsible in the community." [17]

CHAPTER 17

Business and Industry

Business leaders have been interested in human behavior and motivation for many years. At first there was little research, but now a considerable fund of research data has been accumulated. This industrial knowledge about human behavior has generally been ignored by psychologists, psychiatrists, and behavioral scientists. The major reason for this seems to be the high degree of specialization in our society. Psychologists study the work of other psychologists, psychiatrists study psychiatrists. Sociologists develop their own facts. Cross-disciplinary communication has been remarkably poor. Another reason is that much of the data gathered by industry does not meet the exacting specifications of scientific methodology; most of it falls into Maslow's category of proto-knowledge.

From 1927 to 1932 Elton Mayo, Harvard Graduate School of Business Administration, performed the now classic motivational experiments at the Hawthorne Works of Western Electric Company in Chicago. The experiment at Hawthorne started when company engineers tried changing the illumination to increase the productivity of female electrical assemblers. The engineers were astonished to find that whether the lighting was increased, decreased, or held constant, production went up in each of the assembly departments where the experiments were conducted. At this point Mayo and his associates were called in. They continued the experimentation by varying rest periods and the length of the working day. Again, output went up regardless of what they did. The researchers had accidentally uncovered a powerful principle of motivation. Mayo describes it thus: "The major experimental change was introduced when those in charge sought to hold the situation humanly steady . . . by getting the cooperation of the workers. But what actually happened was that six individuals became a team and the team gave itself wholeheartedly and spontaneously to cooperation in the experiment." [1]

Actually, Elton Mayo had uncovered the same phenomena in an earlier study conducted in 1923 in a Philadelphia textile mill. He was seeking to determine the cause of excessive labor turnover in one particular department where work was difficult and monotonous. Assuming the problem was fatigue, he introduced a series of rest periods. The workers were asked to participate in the experiment and help in the scheduling. The results were remarkable: turnover dropped to a level comparable with the rest of the plant, productivity suddenly increased, and morale was noticeably better. Mayo correctly identified the secret as having allowed the employees to participate in decisions usually reserved for management.

Sol W. Gellerman tells about it in his book, *Motivation and Productivity*. "This group moved into a sort of partnership with management rather than into opposition with it. Mayo had thus stumbled upon the very keystone of what later became known as human-relations theory." [1]

Early experiments in human relations did not gain widespread management recognition—managers are, by and large, "practical" men rather than theoretical. Only in the last few years, sparked by the work of Abraham Maslow and a new breed of management consultant, is participative management slowly gaining acceptance. "The theory which he (Mayo) evolved from these studies," says Gellerman, "states that workers tend to cluster together into informal groups in order to fill a void in their lives and that this void results from a basic need for cooperation and comradeship which modern industrial organizations had ignored. Further, these informal groups could exert a far stronger pull on the worker's motivations than the combined strengths of money, discipline, and even job security itself." [1] Mayo recommended finding supervisors skilled in human relations, men who had a natural respect for their fellow men. But he also believed that supervisors could be trained in human-relations skills—communication, listening, and understanding.

In 1960 *Douglas MacGregor*, M.I.T. professor of management and former president of Antioch College, published *The Human Side of Enterprise*.[2] The book stemmed directly from Maslow's new theory of motivation. MacGregor said, "In recent years . . . there has been a convergence of research findings and a growing acceptance of a few rather basic ideas about motivation. These ideas appear to have considerable power . . . they provide the basis for an entirely different theory of management." [2] MacGregor went on to summarize Maslow's hierarchy of basic needs. It was MacGregor's contention that the vast majority of business organizations were ignoring these human needs. He stated they were operating on an obsolete theory which he termed Theory "X". He proposed that management would achieve increased productivity and better worker morale when it understood and dealt with human motivation. He called his approach Theory "Y" management—a philosophy of management which gave workers more freedom, but at the same time more responsibility. This was a type of management that considered the basic needs identified by Dr. Maslow.

"The central principle of organization which derives from Theory "X", states MacGregor, "is that of direction and control through the exercise of authority. . . . The central principle which derives from Theory "Y" is that of integration; the creation of conditions such that the members of the organization can achieve their own goals best by directing their efforts toward the success of the enterprise." [2]

"People, deprived of opportunities to satisfy at work the needs which are now important to them, behave exactly as we might predict—with indolence, passivity, unwillingness to accept responsibility, resistance to change, willingness to follow the demagogue, unreasonable demands for economic benefits." [2]

MacGregor's ideas did not gain immediate acceptance from the business community, but today there is a growing realization that his ideas are valuable. Many advanced students of management consider his work central to the understanding of professional management.

Harwood Manufacturing Corporation is an Eastern firm which manufactures men's pajamas. Alfred J. Marrow, chairman of the board, received his Ph.D. in psychology from New York University and has been a pioneer in applying motivational theory to the industrial situation. Under Marrow's direction Harwood has achieved considerable success in its industry. He says of the corporation's management philosophy, "Harwood's management has been convinced that a job is done best when employees feel that their needs are considered in a way that sustains their self-respect and creates a sense of responsibility. As employees they 'participate'. They do not feel the humiliation implied in the term 'hired hands'." [3] Harwood has been experimenting with effective human relations since 1939, with Professor Kurt Lewin as management consultant. In the late 1940's one of the Harwood plants was making a number of changes in equipment and methods. The changes required that a number of workers be transferred to new tasks and different departments. The result was resistance and resentment, expressed in complaints, resignations, low output, and aggression toward management. Therefore, the management decided to experiment with different approaches to making these necessary work changes. With Lewin's assistance, three similar groups of employees were established.

Group 1 was called into conference and told what their new duties and methods would be. After supervision had explained all of the details, the employees were given the opportunity to ask questions about what had been said.

Group 2 was permitted to choose representatives to work with management to study the problem and determine new methods and procedures. The group representatives first met with management to hear details of the problem. Then they explained the problem to the other workers and returned to management with their viewpoints and suggestions. After helping to make the needed decisions, the representatives explained the plans to their fellow workers.

In Group 3 all the workers were invited to participate with management in deciding on the necessary new methods and procedures.

Here are the production results: For Group 1 production dropped 35% after the changes were made and did not improve for a month. Morale was poor and hostility toward management was evident. 9% of the operators quit within two weeks. A number of others filed grievances about pay rates (pajama workers are paid a minimum rate plus piecework bonus). Group 2 adapted to the changes very rapidly and morale was good. Fourteen days after the changeover the group members achieved standard rates of production, and, by the end of the month, productivity was higher than it was before the changes. No one quit. The same manager who was receiving considerable criticism from Group 1 was getting cooperation from Group 2. Group 3, which used full worker-management participation, performed significantly better than the other two groups. The workers were back to their former level of production on the second day and production continued to increase until it was 14 % higher than ever before. There was excellent morale and the group worked as a team; not one worker quit. The performance of Group 1 was so poor that it had to be broken up after six weeks, but was then reassembled and assigned new duties. This time the change was made using full worker participation. Now, the same workers who were so antagonistic and uncooperative in the Group 1 experiment rapidly adjusted to their new tasks. Morale was high, output excellent, and no one resigned. "This experiment," says Dr. Marrow, "demonstrates that the success of a modern enterprise depends upon motivating the people in the enterprise to accept responsibility, to work together, and thus maximize their performance and their own well being." [3]

Weldon Manufacturing Corporation offers an excellent example of an organization which changed from Theory "X" to Theory "Y" management. The change in management philosophy was carefully documented, not by one observer but by several, all of whom were well grounded in scientific procedures.

In the early 1940's Weldon was one of the fastest growing manufacturers of quality pajamas in the country. By the end of World War II the company was recognized as a leader in its industry. It continued to grow at a steady rate until, by 1955, it was employing about 3,500 people. But the two men who managed Weldon continued to operate the company exactly as they had in the beginning, making all the major decisions themselves. This authoritarian style of management, which had worked so well in the early years, now began to contribute to the decline of the company. One partner was in charge of merchandising, the other in charge of manufacturing. The two owners were ambitious, self-made men who made their own decisions and seldom consulted others. Both were poor at delegation or communication of plans and objectives. As a result the decision-making process was highly centralized. Weldon began losing momentum because of the inflexibility of its leadership. It dropped to 1,000 employees and, in 1962, was acquired by its leading competitor, Harwood Manufacturing Corporation.

The two organizations were similar in many respects. Both were manufacturing pajamas, although for different customers. Both employed about one thousand employees and used similar machinery and methods. But Harwood was using the most advanced methods of professional leadership —participative management—and the corporation was making 17 % on its capital investment while Weldon was losing 15%. The new owners found the management of Weldon to be bureaucratic, authoritarian, and inflexible. As a result, the attitudes of the employees were indifference, hostility, and suspicion; and turnover and absenteeism were extremely high. Performance was low in quantity and quality.

Harwood executives launched a program to change the management philosophy of Weldon. They engaged Drs. Bowers and Seashore from the Institute for Social Research, University of Michigan (headed by Dr. Rensis Likert) and several other management consultants to cooperate in the development program. The conditions existing at Weldon when acquired and the history of the change process were carefully documented by the Institute for Social Research. Employee attitudes and behavior as well as corporate performance were measured and analyzed throughout the project.

In the beginning the employee attitudes in the two companies were quite different. Nearly half the employees of Weldon were thinking of quitting while for Harwood the figure was 17 %. Average monthly turnover at Weldon was 10%, fourteen times higher than Harwood's ¾%. And the monthly rate of absenteeism, at 6%, was double that at Harwood.

The first changes to be made were technical. Some Weldon equipment was obsolete, all was poorly maintained and poorly laid out. The new owners hoped that these changes would in themselves bring considerable improvement in production. However, in spite of significant technical im-

provements, worker productivity remained low, and there was little improvement in morale. It seemed apparent that increased production was
being blocked by the fear and suspicion of the Weldon employees.

Then programs were initiated to change the methods and attitudes of
managers and workers. One of the original partners was gone and the
other soon left, but, except in the sales organization, Harwood kept nearly
all existing managers and employees. Slowly and painfully, the Weldon
managers were taught participative management, almost the exact opposite of that to which they were accustomed. Instead of receiving com-
mands from above, which they were expected to carry out diligently without questioning and pass on in the same manner to those below, executives
now were exposed to the team approach. Decisions were made by groups
of managers working together and coordinating the activities of various
departments. Each manager had far more authority than he had before,
but he also had more responsibility. Communication, instead of moving
mostly downward, now moved up, down, and laterally. Men who had
been frustrated because their ideas were never heard or solicited now had
the opportunity to put first-hand knowledge of their work into play. Starting with plant managers, and then working down in the organization,
Weldon people were exposed to sensitivity training. These training sessions were held away from the plant, usually four days in duration, and
involved people who normally worked together. Participants were taught
to assume greater responsibility and to communicate more fully with their
associates. Many of the participants found it a highly significant experience. It increased their understanding of themselves and others and gave
them new confidence as supervisors. After sensitivity training, managers
were asked to evaluate the results. Here are some typical comments:

"I feel my job is much easier . . . things don't upset me as much as
they did before . . . I get more work done . . . before I went to the
sensitivity sessions my ulcers had been kicking up . . . I haven't had a
single painful attack since." "I am devoting all my energy to my job instead of half-doing it and half-fighting others. I don't feel as though someone is looking over my shoulder and cooking up trouble." "I have been
given more authority than I had before . . . there definitely has also been
a change in my subordinates . . . I guess because I have changed toward
them they act differently toward me." [3]

Workers observed definite changes in their supervisors, too. "There is a remarkable change in them," said one employee, "they have a different attitude toward everything. My boss, particularly, is much calmer, even when something goes wrong. He used to blow his top even when things were normal." "They're much easier to talk to," said another, "Before, I could not talk to certain people too well. They would get angry or sarcastic. Now they seem much calmer and don't get mad as often." [3]

In addition to out-of-plant training, consultants worked directly in the factory to develop better foreman-employee relationships. The same participative problem-solving methods used at the higher levels were now encouraged at the lowest levels. The desired changes did not come easily or rapidly. Employees were not used to being consulted or asked for suggestions regarding improvements in their own procedures. Management had been accustomed to shifting people from job to job and department to department without notice, and frequent layoffs were the rule rather than the exception.

Gradually workers began to appreciate the new climate. "What a welcome change," said one. "This is something Weldon never did before. You have a chance to tell them what you think and you feel you're a part of the company. In the past they told you what to do and you did it." "This is a real switch—to get a chance to express ourselves. Before, if you had a problem and told them about it, they just passed it off and forgot it." [3]

The major changes at Weldon were completed in slightly more than two years. The results recorded by the University of Michigan scientists were highly impressive. Return on invested capital which had been minus 15% at the beginning was now a healthy plus 17%. Production efficiency, measured by industry-wide standards, went from 89% of standard to 114%. The improvement in worker morale was demonstrated by the decrease in monthly turn-over from the original 10% to approximately 4%, and absenteeism diminished to half the previous rate. Manufacturing rejects and scrap loss had been very high at Weldon, but were reduced 39% by the change program, and customer rejects dropped 57%. What happened at Weldon Manufacturing is an impressive demonstration of the importance of sound human relations. The assumptions about human behavior were closely related to the Third Force theories of Abraham Maslow.

In mid-1969, four and one-half years after completion of the organizational change at Weldon, Dr. Bowers and Seashore, who had observed and recorded the change program, made a follow-up study to see if early benefits had continued. They surveyed the attitudes of production employees. Table I, below, summarizes the 1969 employee reactions and compares them to the previous survey before the changed program in 1962 and at the end of the organizational change in 1964. "The general picture," writes Dr. Seashore, "is one of the maintenance of earlier gains in the favorability of employee attitude, or the further improvement in attitudes. This observation holds for seven of the nine indicated." [4]

TABLE I

Changes in job attitudes at the Weldon Plant

	1962 %	1964 %	1969 %
Company better than most	22	28	36
Own work satisfying	77	84	91
Satisfied with pay system	22	27	28
Co. tries to maintain earnings	26	44	41
Satisfied with supervisor	64	54	54
Like fellow employees	85	86	85
Group cohesiveness	25	25	30
Plan to stay indefinitely	72	87	66
Expect future improvement in situation	23	31	43

Business profits between 1964 and 1969 had continued to improve. The Michigan University scientists concluded that the over-all results of their analysis indicated a strong tendency toward stability in the new methods introduced at the Weldon plant. Their report states that "The Weldon organization, far from reverting to its prior condition has during recent years made additional progress toward the organizational goals envisioned by the owners and managers in 1962. . . ." [4]

Rensis Likert, Ph.D., is director of the University of Michigan Institute for Social Research. The Institute is one of the largest behavior research organizations in the nation. Since 1947 the Institute has conducted extensive research in the field of organizational management covering a wide variety of industries, hospitals, government, and even women's clubs. The research, involving many thousand employees and their supervisors, disclosed consistent differences between highly productive managers and low producers. The high producers were found to be what Likert describes as "Employee-centered" while the less productive managers were what he called "job-centered." He states, "Those supervisors whose units have a relatively poor production record tend to concentrate on keeping their subordinates busily engaged in going through a specific work cycle in a prescribed way and at a satisfactory rate as determined by time standards. . . . Supervisors with the best records of performance focus their primary attention on the human aspects of their subordinates' problems and on endeavoring to build effective work groups with high performance goals." [5] The job-centered supervisor does not really understand his employee or how to motivate him. His point of view is similar to that of a supervisor who said, "This interest-in-people approach is all right, but it's a luxury. I've got to keep pressure on for production, and when I get production up, then I can afford to take time to show an interest in my employees and their problems." [5]

In contrast, the high-producing manager has the following attitude: "One way in which we accomplish a high level of production is by letting people do the job the way they want to so long as they accomplish the objective. I believe in letting them take time out from the monotony. Make them feel that they are something special, not just the run-of-the-mill. As a matter of fact, I tell them if you feel that the job is getting you down, get away from it for a few minutes. . . . If you keep employees from feeling hounded, they are apt to put out the necessary effort to get the work done in the required time. . . . If people know their jobs I believe in letting them make decisions. I believe in delegating decision-making." [5]

Highly productive managers have the confidence and respect of their workers and, because of their skills in human relationships, receive greater cooperation and productivity from their workers. Highly-motivated workers have greater freedom, more respect and consideration, greater participation in decision-making, and are part of an enthusiastic and cooperative team. Dr. Likert's research is described in his *New Patterns of Management* (1961).

Chris Argyris, Ph.D., is Professor of Administrative Sciences at Yale University. He has collected an impressive array of data, lending support to Maslow's Third Force theory. "It is the study of relatively healthy individuals," states Argyris, "that resulted in the new emphasis on man's responsibilities and commitments. . . . There is an increasing number of psychologists who believe that self-esteem, self-acceptance, and psychological success are some of the most central factors that constitute individual mental health in our culture. If we are able to understand better how one may enhance the opportunity for individual psychological success, we believe that this will contribute toward individual mental health." [6]

The president of an electronic manufacturing company challenged Dr. Argyris to prove his contention that the average worker was giving the company only about a third of his full capability. Argyris set up a one year experiment in which twelve female electronic assemblers were given individual responsibility for assembling an entire electronic unit. Instead of efficiency experts telling the assemblers how to do the job, they were free to develop their own methods. Furthermore, each of the twelve girls was to inspect the finished product, sign her name to the product, and then handle related correspondence and complaints from customers.

The first month of the experiment was not encouraging. Productivity dropped 30% below that of the traditional assembly-line method, and worker morale was also low. It was not until the end of the eighth week that production started up. But by the fifteenth week production was higher than ever before, and overhead costs of inspection, packing, supervision, and engineering were way down. Production continued significantly higher than that of assembly-line methods for the balance of the one year experiment. Rework costs dropped 94%, and customer complaints dropped from 75% a year to only 3%.

The experiment was ended, but the corporation president (who prefers to remain anonymous) was convinced of its effectiveness, and now is working to utilize the new methods throughout his organization. When the twelve girls were returned to the routine assembly line, three of them were relieved by the decrease in responsibility. The remaining nine found it hard to adjust to the old routine; they missed the challenge of greater freedom with greater responsibility.

Dr. Argyris writes, "With the physical needs of most employees long since assured, the worker seeks to fulfill his next higher order of needs, for security and stability. When these needs become relatively assured, the worker turns toward his highest needs, creativity and self-fulfillment. Precisely because the U.S. has gone further in helping employees fulfill their physical and security needs, it becomes all the more urgent that the industrial structure be adopted to satisfy their higher needs. Ironically the problem is just as urgent on the executive and managerial level as it is on the production line." [7]

Dr. Argyris cites a Yale-sponsored study of 165 top-level executives from ten blue chip corporations. Ninety-five of these executives believed that "responsibility, risk-taking and trust are crucial factors in building a top management team." [7] They considered skills in dealing with people of paramount importance for executives, and yet when these men's executive behavior was examined, it revealed a serious gap between their beliefs and their actual behavior. "Here," says Argyris, "executives as a group show relatively low competence. Furthermore, ministers, professors, architects, doctors, even diplomats suffer as much as business men—often more so." [7] Argyris reports an international study, which covered 5,000 executives in fourteen different countries, which revealed that most of these executives believe that people should be treated with respect and dignity and given as much responsibility as possible. Yet these same executives revealed little understanding of how this might be done.

The management of *Non-linear Systems* has applied Maslow's basic-needs theory since 1960. This is the company that Maslow studied in the summer of 1962 and the source of inspiration for his book *Eupsychian Management*. Non-linear manufactures digital voltmeters in rigorous competition with about 30 other companies. Andrew Kay, Non-linear president and majority stockholder, got his ideas from reading the work of such men as Maslow, Likert, MacGregor, and Drucker. He decided to give these ideas a thorough test and, with this decision, abandoned many assumptions about human nature, which business executives have been making for years. He threw out the assembly-line approach and divided production workers into teams of three to nine people. Each team had a great deal of independence, and the members learned the entire assembly process, including calibration and testing. Said Kay, "Responsibility for quality is placed where we feel it should be—upon the individual making the instrument. . . . We regard management as basically an affair of teaching and training, not one of directing and controlling. We control the process, not the people." [8] The small group approach was chosen because of its ability to fulfill human needs. Arthur Kuriloff, Non-linear Vice President says, "Gregariousness, affiliation, belonging—all these human needs are served in the group." [8]

Time clocks were abandoned, as were regular coffee breaks. Workers took a break whenever it was convenient. Salesmen were not required to submit detailed expense reports. Instead, they were given a reasonable allowance which they could use or not as they saw fit and pocket the difference. They were accountable for the results they produced. The philosophy of greater freedom with greater responsibility was carried throughout the organization. Vance Packard, describing Non-linear in an article for *Reader's Digest,* said, "Andrew F. Kay has staked his company's future on the belief that ordinary people have great potentialities for growth and will perform far better if they are trusted with important responsibilities." [9]

Dr. Richard Farson, president of Western Behavioral Sciences Institute, observed that the first result of the experiment was to boost morale sky high and completely disrupt production. It took three months to get production back to the level produced on the assembly line. Within the next three years, company sales increased 100 %. Productivity per worker went up approximately 30%, while employee turnover dropped to 1/4 the national average, and customer complaints dropped more than 70 %. An unexpected bonus was increased corporate flexibility. New models, which used to take eight or ten weeks to develop, are now out in two or three.

The *American Institute of Management* is one of the Nation's leading management associations. The Institute has analyzed the performance of thousands of business organizations. Their observations regarding the personal qualifications of outstanding business executives provide an interesting confirmation of some of Dr. Maslow's ideas regarding self-actualization. These are the comments of AIM president, Lloyd Marquis. "Out of our years of conducting management audits and repeatedly analyzing the management of thousands of companies, AIM has arrived at some insights that we think are important enough to pass on." [10] Mr. Marquis goes on to explain that excellent managers consistently show a greater respect for people as people and understand people's needs, which he describes as: "self-respect, self-realization, maximum autonomy, recognition, approval, love, respect, and an excess of positive over negative gratifications. . . . They have," he says, "a deep and realistic understanding of human nature and motivation." [10] He states that, compared with the average manager, outstanding managers consistently are more sensitive to moral values and have the "ability to make discriminating judgments, and a great sense of fairness of what is due to each." [10] Excellent managers "delight in the process of achievement." [10] Of average managers he says, "most men who do achieve a major part of their goals have a tendency to feel that they are then entitled to relax and enjoy the fruits of their efforts and ability, while the outstanding managers having achieved one set of goals, adopt new and more advanced ones, and renew their efforts to achieve. Such men find satisfaction not so much in arriving as in the struggle to arrive; past achievement never becomes, for them, as satisfying as present and future achievement. These men seem to be relatively youthful and full of zest at comparatively advanced ages. They delight in the process of achievement." [10]

A recent business survey (1969) reveals the increasing influence of Third Force psychology in industry. The survey was conducted by the *National Industrial Conference Board,* a business-financed research organization, and covered a random sample of North American companies in 21 different categories. A total of 302 organizations responded and of those responding 241 or 80% reported some degree of interest in the behavioral sciences. "The majority of firms," says the report, "say that the behavioral sciences bring new and valuable insight to management and add to productivity and profitability, but that more developmental research is needed." [11] When the survey respondents were asked to name the particular behavioral scientists who had been most influential to them, the list included 202 names. But six names stood out in that they were listed by at least 50 respondents. They were: Douglas MacGregor, mentioned by 134 survey respondents; Frederick Herzberg, 96 mentions; Rensis Likert, 88 mentions; Chris Argyris, 85 mentions; Abraham Maslow, 54 mentions; and Robert Blake and Jane Mouton (developers of the managerial grid process), 52 mentions.[11] Of the top four, all but Herzberg have acknowledged Maslow's Third Force theory and its relationship to their findings.

NOTES & BIBLIOGRAPHY

Chapter 1

1. Mowrer, O. Hobart, "Symposium on Science; Society and the Public's Health —Ethical Issues," Johns Hopkins University, 1966.
2. LaPiere, Richard, *The Freudian Ethic*, Duell, Sloan & Pierce, New York, 1959.
3. Freud, Sigmund, *On Creativity and the Unconscious*, Harper & Row, New York, 1958.
4. Hall, Calvin S. and Gardner Lindzey, *Theories of Personality*, John Wiley & Sons, London, 1957.
5. Maslow, Abraham H., *Motivation and Personality*, Harper & Row, New York, 1954.
6. Freud, Sigmund, *New Introductory Lectures on Psychoanalysis*, W. W. Norton, 1933.
7. Brown, J. A. B., *Freud and the Post-Freudians*, Cassell, 1963.
8. Watson, John B., *Behaviorism*, University of Chicago Press, 1930.
9. Matson, Floyd, *The Broken Image*, Doubleday, New York, 1966.

Chapter 2

1. Hall, Mary Harrington, "A Conversation with Abraham H. Maslow," *Psychology Today*, July, 1968.

2. Maslow, Abraham H., "Music Education and Peak-Experiences," *Music Educators Journal*, 1968.

3. ———, Personal letter to Frank Goble, September 11, 1968.

4. ———, *Motivation and Personality*, Harper & Row, New York, 1954.

5. ———, *Toward a Psychology of Being*, Van Nostrand, New York, 1962.

6. ———, *Eupsychian Management*, Irwin-Dorsey, Illinois, 1965.

7. ———, Personal letter to Frank Goble, February 6, 1968.

8. ———, "Neurosis as a Failure of Personal Growth," *Humanitas*, 1967.

9. ———, *The Psychology of Science*, Harper & Row, New York, 1966.

Chapter 3

1. Maslow, Abraham H., *Motivation and Personality*, Harper & Row, New York, 1954.

2. ———, *Toward a Psychology of Being*, Van Nostrand, New York, 1962.

3. ———, "The Need to Know and the Fear of Knowing," *The Journal of General Psychology*, 1965, 68.

4. ———, "The Creative Attitude," *The Structurist*, No. 3, Saskatoon, 1963.

5. ———, *Eupsychian Management*, Irwin-Dorsey, Illinois, 1965.

6. ———, *New Knowledge in Human Values*, Harper & Row, New York, 1959.

Chapter 4

1. Maslow, Abraham H., *Motivation and Personality*, Harper & Row, New York, 1954.

2. ———, "Isomorphic Interrelationships Between Knower and Known," *Sign, Image, Symbol*, George Braziller, Inc., New York, 1965.

3. ———, *Toward a Psychology of Being*, Van Nostrand, New York, 1962.

4. Zipf, George Kingsley, *Human Behavior and the Principle of Least Effort*, Hafner Publishing Co., New York and London, 1965.

5. Maslow, Abraham H., "Farther Reaches of Human Nature," lecture under auspices of the Esalen Institute, September 14, 1967 in San Francisco.

6. Montagu, Ashley, *The Humanization of Man*, The World Publishing Company, Cleveland and New York, 1962.

7. Maslow, Abraham H., "Toward a Humanistic Biology," unpublished series of memoranda written at the request of the Director of the Salk Institute of Biological Studies, 1968.

Chapter 5

1. Otto, Herbert, The National Center for the Exploration of Human Potential (a preliminary prospectus).

2. Maslow, Abraham H., *Motivation and Personality*, Harper & Row, New York, 1954.

3. ———, *Toward a Psychology of Being*, Van Nostrand, New York, 1962.
4. ———, "Neurosis as a Failure of Personal Growth," *Humanitas*, 1967.
5. ———, "Music Education and Peak-Experiences," *Music Educators Journal*, 1968.
6. ———, "Lessons from the Peak Experiences," *Journal of Humanistic Psychology*, 2, 1962.
7. James, William, *The Varieties of Religious Experience*, Modern Library, 1943.

Chapter 6

1. Maslow, Abraham H., *Toward a Psychology of Being*, Van Nostrand, New York, 1962.
2. ———, "Neurosis as a Failure of Personal Growth," *Humanitas*, 1967.
3. ———, *The Psychology of Science*, Harper & Row, New York, 1966.
4. ———, *Eupsychian Management*, Irwin-Dorsey, Illinois, 1965.
5. ———, *Motivation and Personality*, Harper & Row, New York, 1954.
6. ———, "A Theory of Metamotivation," *Journal of Humanistic Psychology*, VII, 2, 1967.

Chapter 7

1. Maslow, Abraham H., *Motivation and Personality*, Harper & Row, New York, 1954.
2. ———, *Toward a Psychology of Being*, Van Nostrand, New York, 1962.
3. ———, "Adolescence and Juvenile Delinquency in Two Different Cultures," *Festschrift for Gardner Murphy*, Harper, New York, 1960.
4. ———, *Eupsychian Management*, Irwin-Dorsey, Illinois, 1965.
5. ———, "Neurosis as a Failure of Personal Growth," *Humanitas*, 1967.
6. ———, "The Need to Know and the Fear of Knowing," *The Journal of General Psychology*, 68, 1965.
7. ———, "Music Education and Peak-Experiences," *Music Educators Journal*, 1968.
8. ———, *The Psychology of Science*, Harper & Row, New York, 1966.
9. ———, "Isomorphic Interrelationships Between Knower and Known," *Sign, Image, Symbol*, George Braziller, Inc., New York, 1965.

Chapter 8

1. Maslow, Abraham H., *Motivation and Personality*, Harper & Row, New York, 1954.
2. ———, "Neurosis as a Failure of Personal Growth," *Humanitas*, 1967.
3. ———, *Toward a Psychology of Being*, Van Nostrand, New York, 1962.
4. ———, *Eupsychian Management*, Irwin-Dorsey, Illinois, 1965.

5. ———, *The Psychology of Science,* Harper & Row, New York, 1966.
6. ———, "The Need to Know and the Fear of Knowing," *The Journal of General Psychology,* 68, 1965.
7. ———, "Isomorphic Interrelationships Between Knower and Known," *Sign, Image, Symbol,* George Braziller, Inc., New York, 1965.

Chapter 9

1. Maslow, Abraham H., *Motivation and Personality,* Harper & Row, New York, 1954.
2. ———, *Toward a Psychology of Being,* Van Nostrand, New York, 1962.
3. ———, *Eupsychian Management,* Irwin-Dorsey, Illinois, 1965.

Chapter 10

1. Maslow, Abraham H., *Religions, Values and Peak Experiences,* Ohio State University Press, Ohio, 1964.
2. ———, "Eupsychia—the Good Society," *Journal of Humanistic Psychology,* I, 2, 1961.
3. ———, *Toward a Psychology of Being,* Van Nostrand, New York, 1962.
4. ———, *Motivation and Personality,* Harper & Row, New York, 1954.
5. ———, "Fusions of Facts and Values," *American Journal of Psychoanalysis,* 23, 1963.
6. ———, *New Knowledge in Human Values,* Harper & Row, New York, 1959.
7. ———, *Eupsychian Management,* Irwin-Dorsey, Illinois, 1965.
8. ———, Personal interview of Dr. Maslow by Peggy Granger, Menlo Park, California, August, 1969.

Chapter 11

1. Maslow, Abraham H., *Eupsychian Management,* Irwin-Dorsey, Illinois, 1965.
2. Drucker, Peter, *Principles of Management,* Harper & Row, New York, 1954.
3. McGregor, Douglas, *The Human Side of Enterprise,* McGraw-Hill, New York, 1960.

Chapter 12

1. Maslow, Abraham H., *Toward a Psychology of Being,* Van Nostrand, New York, 1962.
2. ———, *Motivation and Personality,* Harper & Row, New York, 1954.
3. ———, *Eupsychian Management,* Irwin-Dorsey, Illinois, 1965.

4. ———, "Music Education and Peak-Experiences," *Music Educators Journal*, 1968.
5. ———, "Fusions of Facts and Values," *American Journal of Psychoanalysis*, 23, 1963.

Chapter 13

1. Maslow, Abraham H., "Synergy in the Society and in the Individual," *Journal of Individual Psychology*, 20, 1964.
2. Murphy, Gardner, *Human Potentialities*, Basic Books, New York, 1958.

Chapter 14

1. Maslow, Abraham H., "Some Educational Implications of the Humanistic Psychologies," *Harvard Educational Review*, Fall, 1968.
2. Jung, C. K., *La Guerison Psychologique*, Librairie de l'Université, Georg et Cie, Geneva.
3. Allport, Gordon, *The Person in Psychology*, Beacon Press, Boston, 1968.
4. Rogers, Carl, *On Becoming a Person*, Houghton Mifflin, Boston, 1961.
5. Hall, Calvin S. and Gardner Lindzey, *Theories of Personality*, John Wiley & Sons, New York, 1957.
6. Hilton, Frank, Personal letter to Frank Goble, March 19, 1968.
7. Assagioli, Roberto, "Psychosomatic Medicine and Bio-Psychosynthesis," pamphlet of lecture given in Rome, September, 1967, PRF Pamphlet no. 5.
8. Cooper, Jack, M.D. and Frank Hilton, "The Will and Will Training," *Psychosynthesis Seminars*, New York, 1966.
9. Low, Abraham, *Mental Health Through Will Training*, The Christopher House, Boston, 1950, 1962.
10. *Los Angeles Times*, November, 1969.
11. Link, Henry C., *The Rediscovery of Man*, Macmillan Co., New York, 1938.
12. Link, Henry C., *The Return to Religion*, Macmillan Co., New York, 1938.
13. Mowrer, O. Hobart, *The Crisis in Psychiatry & Religion*, Van Nostrand, New York, 1961.
14. ———, "The Community Mental Health Concept, Today's Challenge, Tomorrow's Promise," *The Dis-Coverer*, 3, 2, 1966.
15. ———, "Symposium on Science, Society and the Public's Health, Ethical Issues," Johns Hopkins University, 1966.
16. Mainord, Willard A., *Therapy 52—the Truth*, to be published in a Handbook of Direct and Behavior Therapies.
17. ———, "The Visible Defect," chapter for professional book on behavior change.
18. ———, A Therapy, speech presented at Western Psychological Association annual meeting, San Francisco, 1962.

19. Glasser, William, *Reality Therapy*, Harper & Row, New York, 1965.
20. LeShan, Lawrence L., "Changing Trends in Psychoanalytically Oriented Psychotherapy," *Mental Hygiene*, 46, 3, July, 1962.
21. Abt, L. E. and B. F. Riess (eds.), *Progress in Clinical Psychology*, Grune & Stratton, New York, 1966.
22. Bugental, James F. T., "The Third Force in Psychology," *Journal of Humanistic Psychology*, IV, 1, Spring, 1964.
23. ———, *Challenges of Humanistic Psychology*, McGraw-Hill, New York, 1967.

Chapter 15

1. Sands, Bill, *The Seventh Step*, New American Library, New York, 1967.
2. MacDougald, Dan, "A Working Answer to Criminality," Yonan Codex publication, Atlanta, Georgia.
3. ———, "Theological Considerations on the Foundation Method," Yonan Codex publication, Atlanta, Georgia.
4. ———, "Yonan Codex Alcoholic Program," Yonan Codex publication, Atlanta, Georgia.
5. Patten, Tom, "Synanists Play Self-Growth Game," *The Dis-Coverer*, 4, 3, July, 1967.
6. Maslow, Abraham H., *The Psychology of Science*, Harper & Row, New York, 1966.
7. Deitch, David, Daniel Casriel, "New Success in Cure of Narcotics Addicts," *The Physicians Panorama*, October, 1966.
8. ———, "The Role of the Ex-addict in Treatment of Addiction," *Federal Probation*, December, 1967.
9. Ramirez, Efren, "Drug Addiction is Not Physiolotic," *Medical World News*, 1968.

Chapter 16

1. James, Henry, ed., *The Letters of William James*, Atlantic Monthly Press, Boston, n.d.
2. Otto, Herbert, *Group Methods Designed to Actualize Human Potential: a Handbook*, Achievement Motivation Systems, 1968.
3. ———, "The National Center for the Exploration of Human Potential—a Preliminary Prospectus."
4. ———, "Motivation and Human Potentialities," *Humanitas*, III, 3, Winter, 1968.
5. ———, *Human Potentialities*, Warren H. Green, Inc., St. Louis, 1968.
6. Boyle, John, "The Executive-Power Seminar," Executive Dynamics Foundation.

7. Fadiman, James and Richard Katz, "Transformations: the Meaning of Personal Growth," book under preparation, Brandeis University.
8. Glasser, William, *Schools Without Failure,* Harper & Row, New York, 1969.
9. Coopersmith, Stanley, *The Antecedents of Self-Esteem,* W. H. Freeman, San Francisco, 1967.
10. Wood, Benjamin D., Personal letter to Frank Goble, January 31, 1967.
11. Flickinger, Alice, *Indiana Social Studies Quarterly,* XVIII, 3, Winter, 1965–1966.
12. Frankl, Viktor E., "Self Transcendence as a Human Phenomenon," *Journal of Humanistic Psychology,* VI, 2, 1966.
13. Baird, George H., *Greater Cleveland Social Science Program, Handbook for Social Science Teachers,* Educ. Research Council of Greater Cleveland, 1965.
14. Maslow, Abraham H., *Religions, Values and Peak Experiences,* Ohio State University Press, Columbus, 1964.
15. Mayer, Herbert C., speech at annual meeting of the National Council for Social Studies, St. Louis, Mo., November 28, 1964.
16. ———, *The Good American Program—a Teachers' Guide,* Council for Citizenship Education, American Viewpoint, Inc., New York.
17. Trevitt, Virginia, *The American Heritage,* McNally & Loftin, Santa Barbara, 1964.

Chapter 17

1. Gellerman, Sol, *Motivation and Productivity,* American Management Association, New York, 1963.
2. McGregor, Douglas, *The Human Side of Enterprise,* McGraw-Hill, New York, 1960.
3. Marrow, Alfred J., David G. Bowers, and Stanley E. Seashore, *Management by Participation,* Harper & Row, New York, 1967.
4. Seashore, Stanley and David G. Bowers, "The Durability of Organizational Change," presidential address presented by Seashore at the annual meeting of the Division of Industrial Psychology, American Psychological Association, to be published in *The American Psychologist.*
5. Likert, Rensis, *New Patterns of Management,* McGraw-Hill, New York, 1961.
6. Argyris, Chris, *Integrating the Individual and the Organization,* John Wiley & Sons, New York, 1964.
7. ———, "We Must Make Work Worthwhile," *Life,* May 5, 1967.
8. Kuriloff, Arthur, "No Assembly Line Gets Nothing but Results," *Steel,* May 25, 1964.
9. Packard, Vance, "A Chance for Everyone to Grow," *Reader's Digest,* November, 1963.

10. Marquis, Lloyd, "What Makes Them Excellent," *Manual of Excellent Managements,* American Institute of Management, New York, 1965.
11. Rush, Harold M. F. and Walter S. Wikstrom, "The Reception of Behavioral Science in Industry," The National Industrial Conference Board *Record,* 1969.

ACKNOWLEDGMENTS

Acknowledgment is hereby made to Abraham H. Maslow and the publishers of the following books and articles for their permission to reprint quotations in this book:

"The Need to Know and the Fear of Knowing," *The Journal of General Psychology,* 1965, 68; *Eupsychian Management,* copyright © 1965 by Irwin-Dorsey Inc., by permission of the publisher; *Toward a Psychology of Being,* Second Edition, by Abraham H. Maslow, copyright © 1968 by Litton Educational Publishing, Inc., by permission of Van Nostrand Reinhold Company; *Religions, Values, and Peak Experiences,* by Abraham H. Maslow, copyright © 1964 by Kappa Delta Pi Society, by permission Kappa Delta Pi Society; *Motivation and Personality,* by Abraham H. Maslow, copyright © 1954 by Harper & Row Publishers, Inc., by permission of the publisher; *New Knowledge in Human Values* by Abraham H. Maslow, copyright © 1959 by Harper & Row Publishers, Inc., by permission of the publisher; *The Psychology of Science* by Abraham H. Maslow, copyright © 1966 by Harper & Row Publishers, Inc., by permission of the publisher; "The Creative Attitude" by Abraham H. Maslow, *The Structurist,* No. 3, 1963, University of Saskatchewan, Saskatoon, Canada, by permission of *The Structurist;* "Music Education and Peak-Experiences" by Abraham H. Maslow, *Music Educators Journal,* 1968, 54, by permission of *Music Educators Journal;* "Isomorphic Interrelationships Between Knower and Known," published in *Sign, Image, Symbol,* edited by Gyorgy Kepes, copyright © 1965 by George Braziller, Inc., by permission of the publisher; "Synergy in the Society and in the Individual" by Abraham H. Maslow, *Journal of Individual Psychology,* Vol. 20, November, 1964, by permission of the *Journal of Individual Psychology;* "A Theory of Metamotivation" by Abraham H. Maslow, *Journal of Humanistic Psychology,* VII, 2, 1967 and "Eupsychia—the Good Society" by Abraham H. Maslow, *Journal of Humanistic Psychology,* I, 2, 1961 and "Lessons from the Peak-Experiences" by Abraham H. Maslow, *Journal of Humanistic Psychology*, 1, 1962, by permission of the *Journal of Humanistic Psychology;* "Neurosis as a Failure of Personal Growth" by Abraham H. Maslow, *Humanitas*, 1967, by permission of *Humanitas;* "Fusions of Facts and Values" by Abraham H. Maslow, by permission of the Editor from *The American Journal of Psychoanalysis*, Vol. 23, No. 2, 1963.

Acknowledgment is also made to the authors and publishers of the following books and articles for permission to reprint quotations used in this book: *The Crisis in Psychiatry and Religion* by O. Hobart Mowrer, copyright © 1961, by Litton Educational Publishing, Inc., by permission of Van Nostrand Reinhold Company; *The Humanization of Man* by Ashley Montagu, copyright © 1962 by Ashley Montagu, by permission of The World Publishing Company; *Motivation and Productivity* by Sol Gellerman, copyright © by the American Management Association, Inc., by permission of the publisher; *Behaviorism* by John B. Watson, by permission of W. W. Norton & Company, Inc., copyright 1924, 1925 by John B. Watson, copyright 1930, Revised Edition, by W. W. Norton & Company, Inc., and renewed © 1958 by John B. Watson; *The Antecedents of Self-Esteem* by Stanley Coopersmith, W. H. Freeman and Company, copyright © 1967, by permission of the publisher; *On Becoming a Person* by Carl R. Rogers, copyright © 1961 by Houghton Mifflin Company, by permission of the publishers; "We Must Make Work Worthwhile" by Chris Argyris, *Life* Magazine, May 5, 1967, © 1967 by Time Inc., by permission of the publisher; *The Letters of William James*, Volume II, edited by Henry James, by permission of The Atlantic Monthly Press, Little, Brown and Company; *Human Potentialities* by Herbert A. Otto, copyright © 1968 by Warren H. Green, Inc., by permission of the author and publisher; *Group Methods Designed to Actualize Human Potential: a Handbook* by Herbert A. Otto, Achievement Motivation Systems, 1968, by permission of the author; *The Person in Psychology* by Gordon Allport, copyright © 1968 by The Beacon Press, by permission of the publisher; *New Introductory Lectures on Psychoanalysis* by Sigmund Freud, translated and edited by James Strachey, copyright 1933 by Sigmund Freud, renewed 1961 by W. J. H. Sprott, copyright © 1965, 1964 by James Strachey, with the permission of the publisher, W. W. Norton & Company, Inc.; *The Human Side of Enterprise* by Douglas McGregor, copyright © 1960 by Douglas McGregor, by permission of the publisher, McGraw-Hill Book Co., Inc.; *New Patterns of Management* by Rensis Likert, copyright © 1961 by Rensis Likert, by permission of the publisher, McGraw-Hill Book Co., Inc.; "Drug Addiction is Not Physiologic" by Efren Ramirez, *Medical World News*, 1968, by permission of *Medical World News; Theories of Personality* by Calvin S. Hall and Gardner Lindzey, copyright © 1957 by John Wiley & Sons, Inc., and *Integrating the Individual and the Organization* by Chris Argyris, copyright © 1964 by John Wiley & Sons, Inc., by permission of the publisher; *Management by Participation* by Alfred J. Marrow, David G. Bowers, and Stanley E. Seashore, by permission of the publisher, Harper and Row Publishers, Inc.; *Reality Therapy* by William Glasser, by permission of the publisher, Harper & Row Publishers, Inc.; *Schools Without Failure* by William Glasser, by permission of the publisher, Harper & Row Publishers, Inc.; *On Creativity and the Unconscious* by Sigmund Freud, by permission of the publisher, Harper & Row Publishers, Inc.; *Progress in Clinical Psychology* by L. E. Abt and D. F. Riess (eds.), Vol. VII, 1966, by permission of the publisher, Grune & Stratton, Inc.; "The Visible Defect" by Willard A.

Mainord, by permission of the author; "Synanists Play Self-Growth Game" by Tom Patton, *The Dis-Coverer*, Vol. 4, No. 3, July, 1967, by permission of Dis-Coverer, Inc.; "The Will and Will Training" by Frank Hilton and Jack Cooper, *Psychosynthesis Seminars*, 1966, by permission of Frank Hilton; "The Third Force in Psychology" by J. T. F. Bugental, *Journal of Humanistic Psychology*, IV, 1, Spring, 1964, by permission of the *Journal of Humanistic Psychology;* "Changing Trends in Psychanalytically Oriented Psychotherapy" by Lawrence L. LeShan, *Mental Hygiene,* Vol. 46, No. 3, July, 1962, by permission of the author and *Mental Hygiene.*

Index

This book was set on the linotype in Caledonia.
The display faces are Caledonia and Perpetua.
Printed by Noble Offset Printers, Inc., New York
Bound by H. Wolff Book Manufacturing Co., New York
Desiged by Jacqueline Schuman.